Madison Clinton Peters

Empty Pews and Selections from other Sermons on timely Topics

Madison Clinton Peters

Empty Pews and Selections from other Sermons on timely Topics

ISBN/EAN: 9783337159689

Printed in Europe, USA, Canada, Australia, Japan

Cover: Foto ©ninafisch / pixelio.de

More available books at **www.hansebooks.com**

/ SELECTIONS FROM OTHER

SERMONS ON TIMELY TOPICS II

BY

MADISON C. PETERS

PASTOR FIRST PRESBYTERIAN CHURCH, PHILADELPHIA

PHILADELPHIA
A. T. ZEISING & CO., PRINTERS AND PUBLISHERS
402, 404 & 406 RACE STREET

TO

REV. J. H. GOOD, D. D.

PRESIDENT OF

HEIDELBERG THEOLOGICAL SEMINARY, TIFFIN, OHIO

THIS BOOK IS AFFECTIONATELY

DEDICATED

AS A TOKEN OF GRATITUDE, BY HIS FORMER STUDENT

THE AUTHOR

PREFACE.

In the midst of a busy pastorate we venture to send forth this book, bespeaking for it the charitable judgment of friends and strangers. The selections are mainly taken from stenographic reports, by Mr. Henry J. Greer, of Sunday evening sermons on timely topics, preached to audiences overflowing in almost each instance the possibilities of the building. We give these homely selections this permanent home in the hope and with the prayer that their influence may be for the good of man and the glory of God.

M. C. P.

December, 1886.

CONTENTS.

CHAPTER.	PAGE.
I.—Empty Pews,	9
II.—America's Most Popular Sin,	20
III.—The Character of Christ,	25
IV.—The Fullness of Time,	28
V.—The Right Vocation,	33
VI.—The Sunday Question,	34
VII.—High-Toned Scoundrelism.	37
VIII.—The Tramp.	39
IX.—Intermarriage,	41
X.—Good Housekeeping.	43
XI.—Unequally Yoked Together,	45
XII.—Beauty.	46
XIII.—"A Friend in Need is a Friend Indeed."	48
XIV.—Revenge.	51
XV.—Grumblers.	52
XVI.—Gossipers,	54
XVII.—Is Christianity Failing?	57
XVIII.—Wanted—A Man,	68
XIX.—Crimes and Criminals,	71
XX.—Dollars and Sense,	75
XXI.—The World Unsatisfying,	77
XXII.—Sensational Preaching,	79
XXIII.—A Sum in Addition,	81
XXIV.—Sleeping Under the Sermon,	86
XXV.—Calvin and Calvinism,	89
XXVI.—The Bible and History,	91

CONTENTS.

CHAPTER.	PAGE.
XXVII.—Pride,	95
XXVIII.—Honoring Our Parents,	98
XXIX.—Hypocritical Punctiliousness,	101
XXX.—The Lawyers,	103
XXXI.—Force of Character,	105
XXXII.—Funeral Reform,	107
XXXIII.—Evolution,	109
XXXIV.—Hell in the Light of Common Sense,	111
XXXV.—That Boy of Yours,	120
XXXVI.—Random Shots,	124

Prudery—The Christian Abroad—Talk and Conversation—Carrying a Revolver—Exaggeration—Low-Necked Dresses—Tight Lacing—Horse-Racing—Ill Temper—True Religion—Busybodies—True Living—The Sensitive Man—Table Prayer—A Cure for Anger—A Good Rule for the Married—Objectors—Little Bad Habits—Parental Indulgence—Affectation—The Education of Woman—Sunlight—Fresh Air—Gambling—Monopolies—The False Witness—False Measures—Marrying for Money—Love is Not All—Trust Not Appearances—Marry The Man—A Warning—What Girls Should Know—Girls' Extravagance—A Wise Choice—Don't—Flirting—The Novel—An Illogical Criticism—Snobbery—Common-Sense Education—A Trade—Coming to Town—One Covenant—Be Progressive—Religion in Business—Original Sin—"The Elect"—The Main Thing—The Atonement—The Jew—The Faithful Servant Girls—Time—Benevolence—Envy—Purity—Christ's Text-Book—Getting On in the World—Prayer—Decision of Character—The Cheap System—Young Man, Beware!—Fancy Pictures—Trust Not Too Far—Companionship with Fools—Silence—"Pay as You Go"—Keep the Children at School—True Blue Blood—Money All Gone—The Christian Character—Borrowing Trouble—Arithmetic—A Base Motto—The Joyous Christian—The Poor—When in Rome—Behind the Age—Honesty and Policy—An Antidote for Frivolity—A False Charity—Hasty Words—Why?—Good-Looking Folks—Heaven Upon Earth—The Frosted Windows—A Sad Fact—Pluck—How to Drive the Children Away from Home—Do Right—"Thou Shalt Not Steal"—Fie for Shame!—Shut Out—A Good Conscience—Sunday and the Workingman—"Ready for Either"—The Commercial Liar—Politics and Religion—A Wish—"Seek Ye the Lord"—Waiting—Inability—Study the Bible—To Business Men—A Word to the Aged—A Fact—Be Your Own Match-Maker—A Bad Mother—Long Life—Loyalty to Conscience—Mirth a Medicine—Tell the Truth—Courtesy to Children—Parting Words.

I.

Empty Pews.

"Brethren my heart's desire and prayer to God for Israel is that they might be saved."—*Romans*, x: 1.

THOUSANDS upon thousands of well-disposed, intelligent, warm-hearted men and women seldom enter the church, except possibly to attend a funeral or witness a wedding. How does it come about that this is so? I will give you, as far as I can in one sermon, my views upon this perplexing problem. I do not know that my views will agree with yours; on such a question difference of opinion is to be expected. The graveness of the subject forbids silence. The pulpit that does not examine the causes of its own weakness, is too incapable to know its duty, or too cowardly to do it.

Now, one reason, as I understand this matter, so many pews are empty, is because of want of pulpit ability. I am not underrating the ministry. The most attentive and regular church-goers do not fall behind me in speaking freely of the dullness, the sameness, the inconsequence, the length of the sermon. A preacher of any but the highest powers who ventures to detain his hearers beyond half an hour, is regarded as a sort of social criminal, and the prospect of an hour's sermon would keep even most of "the regulars" away. Short services and shorter sermons are insisted on by the taste of the day. The impatience of preaching demands serious attention. The clergy may well say: *We have piped unto you, and ye have not danced; we have mourned to you, and ye have not wept.*

A homely but true adage is: "A sermon, like a pudding, must have something in it." We all have heard men preach who would have made as good sportsmen as the Irishman who aimed at nothing, and hit it every time. Good old Andrew Fuller once exclaimed: "Oh, the holiness of their living, and the painfulness of their preaching." The want of brains in a preacher is a capital defect, and no amount of moral and spiritual excellence will make a stupid man a successful preacher. It is not true that the Apostles were ignorant fishermen. If, for instance, the author of the fourth Gospel had been originally an ignorant fisherman, he was something very different when he penned his account of the life of Christ. He is learned in the subtleties of neo-Platonism; he knows the metaphysics of Alexandria; and, unless he wrote down things which he did not understand, we must confess that here we have advanced learning and high and general culture employed in the early propagation of Christian doctrine. Paul stands unequaled to this day as a rhetorician. If high culture and education were necessary in apostolic times to give effect to preaching, how much more necessary must they be now?

It is often said of a man, "He is a good pastor, but no preacher." God sent him to preach. Fifty pastoral visits during the week, sipping tea and nursing babies, will not hold a thinking audience on Sunday. Many ministers have brains enough, but not brains enough to know how practically to use their brains. They leave them at home when they preach.

When Edward Irving published four discourses under the title of "Orations," he gave as the reason that the very word "sermon" was indicative of dullness. A sermon should be a thing of life and beauty. It need not be great, eloquent, magnificent; but instead of dull, drowsy and dry platitudes, flowery and glittering generalities, put something in the sermon to glow, brighten, convince, subdue—"thoughts that breathe and words that burn."

The Gospel affords the grandest theme for genuine eloquence, and the last place on earth one should expect to find dullness ought to be in the pulpit. Our empty pews are in a large measure due to weakness in power of statement, and oratorical inefficiency of the ministry. A preacher asked Garrick, the tragedian, " Why is it you are able to produce so much more effect with the recital of your fictions than we do by the delivery of the most important truths?" "My Lord," said Garrick, "You speak truths as if they were fictions ; we speak fictions as if they were truths." The pulpit depreciates too much the importance of manner as an instrument for doing good. The want of rhetorical culture is admitted to be one of the greatest and most constant causes of failure in the pulpit. The graceful gesture, the modulated voice, the logical clearness, the elegant expression, by appropriate emotion, by graceful action—these things are wonderful aids in sustaining, melting, inflaming and overwhelming our auditors.

Instead of droning, and whining, and canting, and moaning, and croaking, and funeralizing religion, let us freshen up and get out of the old ruts, and introduce into our sermons the brightness, the holy sarcasm, the sanctified wit, the epigrammatic power, the blood-red earnestness and the fire of zeal. Instead of going through our sermons cool, collected and composed, let us surround our pulpits with heaven's fire, and send our hearers away aroused, saying: "This man is in earnest; we must come and hear him again." No life can be above stale mediocrity without the inward glow and passion called *enthusiasm*. Kindled from truth and eternal principles, it is "*God in us.*" Emerson truly remarks, that " Every great and commanding movement in the annals of the world is the triumph of enthusiasm." When on his way to Rome, in 1867, Garibaldi was cast into prison, he wrote to his comrades: "If fifty Garibaldis are thrown into prison, let Rome be free." He did not care for his own comfort so long as the cause of freedom in Italy was advanced. If we had such enthusiasm for our Master and his cause, the prayer put into the disciples' lips by Jesus himself, "*Thy Kingdom Come,*" would be rapidly and gloriously answered. With a bleeding heart I think of the thousands in the temples of sin, and the few in the churches who doze and nod over sermons destitute of fire and evangelical fervor. " Give me only fire enough," said Bernard Palissy, "and these pigments will become indelibly fixed upon this china." His derisive neighbors screamed, " he is mad." "More fire!" shouted the determined man; "more fire!" and to-day the name of Palissy is a synonym for determination and success. I say the same—more fire! more fire! More fire in our sermons, more fire in our preachers, more fire in our prayers and songs, more fire in the pew, more fire in everything we do, and we will forever impress the blessed name of the Lord Christ in the dull, cold hearts of men.

> " Thou must be true thyself,
> If thou the truth wouldst teach;
> Thy soul must overflow, if thou
> Another's soul wouldst reach ;
> It needs the overflow of heart
> To give the lips full speech."

Again, our preaching is *too theologic*. The people are tired of set theological terms and phrases. Terminology and vocabulary people do not understand nor care for. They do not affect nor stir. There is neither force nor application to such preaching. It is like some people's hand-shaking; the hand is good enough, but there is no grip to it. We need less theology and more Christianity —less of Paul and more of Christ—but not Christ as the centre of a mere theology. The life, the character, as they contain and illustrate the life and character of Christ himself, is that which saves the soul. We must have Christ in our lives as well as in our creeds. Such a view of Christianity the people can understand and feel the force of. Life is too short and too valuable to be spent in spinning theological cobwebs and building speculative castles in the air. Christendom is full of star-gazers and sun-gazers; men so wrapped in lunar speculations, or stellar calculations, or solar computations, as to the high sky of religion that they have forgotten man. There are plenty of sermons on justification, verbal inspiration, effectual calling and the efficacy of the sacraments ; but you seldom hear sermons on common honesty, or these primitive commandments : Thou shalt not lie ; Thou shalt not steal ; Thou shalt not commit adultery. All that Christianity is meant to do in making life pure is left undone. Our duty is no longer to be honest and true and self-denying and pure, but to hold accurately the creed of the church.

Instead of telling a Christian congregation every Sunday *to believe in the Lord Jesus Christ*, thus telling them to do what they are already doing, let the Gospel be applied practically to society and the affairs of men. We need ministers of the present, and not mere mouth-pieces of the past. Let us not simply blow a penny whistle, but a trumpet in Zion.

Let us not mouth thundering words about sinners in the mass, and pass by the individual sinners who fill our pews and pay our salaries. Talk about the living Pharisees, and not the Pharisees of Judea, who have been dust and ashes for eighteen hundred years. Shame on the minister who fawns upon the people, flatters them and credits them with virtues which he knows they do not possess; who avoids truth because disagreeable to his hearers; who panders to prejudices in public which in private he despises. The people always rush to hear the man who does not stick and stutter and stammer in telling the truth. The courageous preacher will attract attention, compel conviction and arouse to action. Indeed people will be offended if you tell them the truth. The woman broke the looking-glass because it showed wrinkles in her face. Those who get vexed because sin is aimed at them, do so because they are shot; and woe to the minister who dares to keep his mouth shut when the people sin! I have grown sick at heart over the sycophantic cowardliness of pusillanimous souls in the pulpit. With an earnestness which well-nigh takes my breath away, I plead for a ministry terrible in its earnestness, and uncompromising in its denunciation of sin and wickedness—sparing none. God forbid that the seductive voices and subtle influences of the world should ever charm my lips to silence.

Perhaps the spirit of our age has something to do with empty pews. Theology will always be present tense. Man was made for religion, and until his nature is changed, the foundations of religion will remain unshaken. The human soul was created to look above material nature. It wants a God for its love and trust, an immortality for its hope. It wants the peace of heart and satisfaction of spirit that can only be found in Christ.

The world can never outgrow the need of salvation. The spiritual wants of the race will be the same forever. It is this Gospel alone applied by the Holy Spirit that converts sinners, edifies saints, establishes the church and revolutionizes the world.

Creeds, written statements of belief, are necessary, whether in politics or religion. No progress can be made unless an explicit statement of beliefs and purposes is put before the people. Show me a man who has no creed, either written or unwritten, and I will show you an idiot. But our creeds embody much that is objectionable, if not false, and is one reason why so many men and women do not make a public profession of religion. The creeds of our churches are too inclusive of detail in doctrine and scriptural interpretation, and too exacting and arbitrary in their terminology, so that people cannot give unqualified assent to them. Why should we be led in our theological thinking by men who lived centuries ago?

For instance: The Westminster divines met in 1648. They were appointed as a commission by the Parliament to get together some sort of codification to compose the distracted thought of the time. They met. They were grand Christian men; good men as ever lived before them; good men as have lived since; they did their work as well as they could. And yet that assembly was divided. There were hot discussions, and the things that they carried were carried by a mere majority, with strong protest against them. Shall what they did constitute the spectacles through which we are to look upon our Bible to-day?

"Through the shadow of the globe
We sweep into the younger day."

We have better methods of investigation, and ought to

have a better knowledge of the facts of revelation than our predecessors had, and as we acquire a more accurate knowledge of facts and laws, a rectification of theories must be brought about. I want you, however, distinctly to understand that I have no sympathy with the new-fangled doctrines which some restless teachers of this age would force down our throats, and which are not worth a *dog's dying for them*, much less a man's. I have humbly preached the old truths in new and attractive dress, and I thank God that he has always blessed me with crowded audiences. I am no more a fool than my contemporaries, and if I could see any thing better than these truths I would willingly grasp them. But God forbid that I should glory save in the cross of Christ. I will stand by it as long as I live. Return unto thy rest, oh, my soul! All I ask is, that our creeds be revised, abbreviated, simplified; that the doctrines of the churches be brought up to the level of present needs and present enlightenment on the great question of man's relation to God. And if "revision" did not hurt the Bible, surely creeds, which are only human, would not be hurt by being revised. It is true, our creed is not imposed on our members. No one joining our church is required to subscribe to our articles. Why not have a creed so simple that our members can subscribe to it? If I err on this subject, believe me, my error is of the head and not of the heart.

Disputatious preaching makes empty pews. Too many men preach to maintain their views rather than to win men to Christ. Much preaching is better calculated to make enemies than friends. Bigotry is the enemy which sows arrows, fire-brands and death in the army of the Lord. In the Devil's army one mind rules all. The line is closely set, and its movement as of one man.

The heavenly army is broken up into groups, one leader is slandering another leader, and the privates are throwing stones at their respective captains. God speed the day when all our churches will be heaven-like, to which all denominations go, Jews and Catholics not excepted; and I thank God that He has deemed me worthy to bear His message to such various minds and souls as these.

Stiff preachers make empty pews. The preacher should be the people's man—one of the people. He should prove himself the friend of mankind. He should descend from his pomp and high platform of empty dignity and come amongst the people, speak to the people and show himself a friend of manhood at large, remembering that his Master was the people's Christ.

Cold churches make empty pews. Christianity is served too much on ice. We want warm hearts, warm greetings, warm hand-shakings in all our churches. People meet every Sunday in many of our churches for years, and, in attempting to get up a smile of recognition, they will look like the Egyptian sphinx.

Again, *religion is advertised wrongly*. Religion is not a sullen Stoicism, nor a sour Phariseeism. It does not consist in length of face, in a few melancholy passions, in some dejected looks, or depressions of mind. It is a cold, cheerless, heartless asceticism and not the Christian religion which gives man an unnatural and forbidding appearance. Many a man imagines himself very pious, who has nothing more than dyspepsia. This twisting and perverting God's word into unnecessary rules for the abridgment of Christian liberty and conduct, have done much to drive the liberal-minded, large-hearted, independent and the young people from the church. We want more joy to be brought out of the world by

Christians. The brighter and the merrier the Christian's face, the better for the cause of Christ.

We want more joy in our religion. It is high time we cease singing:

> "Look how we grovel here below,
> Fond of these trifling toys;
> Our souls can neither fly nor go,
> To reach eternal joys,"

et id omne genus humbugibus. Is Christianity the refrain of a lost cause? Or is it not the proclamation of a grand triumph? Almost all prayers are a piteous beseeching, lamentation and depreciation. Men accuse themselves of everything in praying; and should the pastor say "Amen! Lord that is so," the pastor would have to go. "Delight thyself in the Lord." "Rejoice in the Lord alway."

But the most common excuse for staying away from church is: "church-goers are no better than non-church-goers." Now, we will not insult you by giving you figures, but go to our penitentiaries and jails: are there more church-goers than non-church-goers there? Look at the criminals in the police courts to-morrow morning: are they church-goers or non-church-goers? Who are they who work for the elevation and purity of public morals, and to ameliorate the condition of humanity? Church-goers or non-church-goers? To say that the people, as a rule, who go to church are no better as a rule than those who do not go, displays either deplorable ignorance or pitiful bigotry.

It is true that all are not saints who go to church. There are Balaams in the church; in profession prophets of Jehovah; in practice "lovers of the wages of unrighteousness." There are Sunday saints and week-day devils. Hence the necessity of preaching practical righteousness. Let such men be thundered out of the communion of the church.

Brethren, the great want of the present age is not so much arguments sustaining Christianity, as living Christians illustrating and exemplifying it. There is a plenty of sounding brass, and tinkling cymbals are not hard to find. There is hypocrisy enough in the world, and there is no need that Christians should increase it by empty talk and vain profession. They best answer the power of Christ's Gospel, who in their lives exemplify and demonstrate it. Conduct is the great profession. What a man *does* tells us what he *is*. A covetous professor, a quarreling church, a renegade preacher, a dishonest and tricky church official, a corrupt religious corporation, a praying defaulter, a sanctimonious robber of widows and orphans, does more to make men infidels and keep them away from the church, than the most blatant bar-room talker, or the most polished infidel lecturer. The translation of the Bible most needed to-day, is its translation into flesh and blood, into the daily walk, works and words of men, and the world will not be able to resist the evidence of the divine mission of our Lord. Let the light of the knowledge of the glory of God blaze out in the lives of his children, and an astonished world will mark the change, and seek in some way to account for a revelation so wonderful, so transforming.

"Let your light so shine before men, that they may see your good works, and glorify your Father which is in heaven."

II.

America's Most Popular Sin.

AMERICANS are the profanest people in the world. A traveler in Russia was judged to be a clergyman because he was not heard to swear, all other Americans being supposed to be addicted to this wicked practice.

The air is filled with oaths. Turn where you will, you can hear men swear. Young and old, men and women, high and low, rich and poor, learned and illiterate, church members and non-church members, prostitute the name of God to vile and mean uses.

Louis IX. of France, punished any one who was convicted of swearing by searing his lips with a hot iron. If we had such a law in Philadelphia, how the hot iron business would flourish. When some one complained to the King that the punishment was too severe, he replied, "I would to God that by searing my own lips, I could banish out of my realm all abuse of oaths." Chrysostom's remedy was: "Every time, whenever thou shalt forget thyself to have let slip an oath, punish thyself for it by missing the next meal." With such a custom prevailing in our midst, how many boarding houses would flourish?

Now, we have five reasons why the name of God should not be taken in vain :

It is *useless*. Did curses ever start a heavy load? Did they ever unravel a tangled skein? Did they ever take the meanness out of a customer? Did they ever collect a bad debt? Did they ever cure a toothache? *Did they ever accomplish anything?* Verily, the swearer is the silliest of all dealers in sin. He sins gratis. He sells his soul for nothing.

When Job's misfortunes were completed by being himself smitten with boils from head to foot, Mrs. Job, the worst boil he had, virtually said to him: "*Why don't you swear?* Curse God, though you die in so doing." Yet profanity would not have removed one boil, would not have brought back one of the captured animals, nor restored any one of the dead children.

It is *cowardly to swear.* There was once a man who swore dreadfully in the presence of others, but was rebuked by a gentleman, who told him that it was cowardly for him to do in the presence of others that which he did not dare do by himself. "Ah," said the man, "I am not afraid to swear at any time or in any place." "I'll give you ten dollars," said the gentleman, "if you will go in the village graveyard at twelve o'clock to-night and utter the same oaths you have just uttered here, when you are alone with God." "Agreed," said the man; "it's an easy way of earning ten dollars." "Well, you come to me to-morrow, and say that you have done it, and the money is yours." He was impatient for the midnight hour. When the time came he hurried to the graveyard. Darkness and silence were brooding like spirits o'er the still and pulseless world. Beneath him the many dead, above him pitch darkness. The words, "alone with God," came over him with mighty power; a deep sense of his monstrous folly and heinous wickedness fell upon him like the sudden pealing thunder of the midnight storm. His further endeavors were thwarted by the Invisible One. He could go no further. Instead of carrying out his purpose, acting rudely and saucily with God; instead of blistering his mouth with hot and sulphurous oaths, he was humbled, and trembling, cried with a loud voice, "God be merciful to me a sinner." The next day he went to the gentleman and thanked him for what he had done; and said he had resolved never to swear another oath as long as he lived.

To swear is *impolite*. Cowper once wrote:

> "It chills my blood to hear the blest Supreme,
> Lightly appealed to on each trifling theme;
> Maintain your rank; vulgarity despise;
> To swear is neither brave, polite, nor wise."

Can he who leads every sentence with an oath or a curse, wear the name and garb of a gentleman? This reminds me of that incident of Abraham Lincoln, who said to a person sent to him by one of the Senators, and who in conversation uttered an oath: "I thought the Senator had sent me a gentleman. I see I was mistaken. There is the door, and I bid you good-day."

Profanity indicates low breeding. It detracts from the grace of conversation. It is an evidence of a weak brain and limited ideas. I care not what kind of clothes a man wears; what culture he boasts; what refinement he prides in; what family connections he has; how much he may restrain himself in the presence of ladies, he who fears not to rush into the presence of a thrice holy and Almighty God, with oaths upon his lips, is no gentleman. No language can be more disgustful, more grate the ear or fret the heart, than to hear the God of heaven summoned in attestation of tattle, or challenged to damn and destroy.

Swearing is *wicked*. It springs from a mere malignancy of spirit in man against God, because he has forbidden it. As far as the violation of the command of God is concerned, the swearer is equally guilty with the murderer, the unchaste person, the robber and the liar. Whose is this name which men roll off the lips of blasphemy as though they were speaking of some low vagabond. God! Yes, men swear by the name of God. It makes my hair rise, my flesh creep, my blood chill, my breath catch, my foot halt. God! In whose presence the highest and purest seraphim veil their faces, and cry in notes responsive to each other: "Holy! Holy! Holy! Lord God of Hosts!" God! God Almighty! Think! Swearer think! You are guilty of a sin that mounts to heaven with daring, and is hurled back into your blasphemous teeth with withering condemnation. Every star in the heavens flashes rebuke into your face; every quivering leaf, every lurid shaft of lightning, every shock of thunder, all the voices of the tempest, the harping angels, and the very scoffing devils rebuke you. Who will ever again malign the name of God? Is there a hand in this vast congregation to-night that will ever again be lifted to wound him? If so, let that hand, blood-tipped, be lifted now. Which one of you will ever again use his name in imprecation? If any, let them speak. Not one! Not one!

Swearing is a *dangerous* sin. The third commandment is the only one in the decalogue to which is affixed the certainty of punishment: "For the Lord will not hold him *guiltless* that taketh his name in vain." It was a capital offense under the Levitical law (Lev. xx: 10). The New Testament reiterates in paragraph after paragraph and chapter after chapter, that profane swearers are accursed now, and are to be forever miserable. No wonder that this iniquity has so often been visited with the immediate curse of God. Profane swearer, whether you think so or not, your oath is a prayer—an appeal to

God. How frequently the awful imprecations *damn* and *God damn* roll from your profane tongue. Are you really desirous of an answer to your prayer? Be thankful that your prayer has not been awswered.

The oaths that you utter may die on the air, but God hears them, and they have an eternal echo. I beseech you, I conjure you, break off this useless, impolite, cowardly, wicked and dangerous habit ere the brittle thread of life breaks, and you are plunged into eternal misery. Oh! let your oaths be turned into supplications! Repair immediately to the throne of grace, and beg for pardon and mercy. Before you lay down this book, turn to Jesus, who died for swearers as well as for his murderers. And then, oh then, though you may have sworn as many oaths as there are stars in the heavens, and sands upon the sea shore innumerable—then you shall find, to your eternal joy, that there is love in His heart, and merit in his blood, sufficient to pardon your sins and save your soul forever. Swearer, can you ever again blaspheme such a God and Saviour as this? Does not your conscience cry, God forbid? Even so. Amen.

III.
The Character of Christ.

THE more we study the character of Jesus Christ, the more we will fall in love with him. There is no one with whom we can compare him. He is the miracle of the ages, than whom there can be no greater—above all praise and eulogy. He is in the noblest and most perfect sense the realized ideal of humanity.

It is a remarkable fact, that there is no hesitation among the great intellects of different ages: whatever their special position towards Christianity, whether its humble disciples, or those openly opposed to it, or carelessly indifferent, or vaguely latitudinarian, they have uniformly borne testimony to the originality and transcendent excellency of the character of Christ. Thus Josephus, the great Jewish historian, who lived in the latter part of the first century, refers to Christ as *"a wise man, if it be proper to speak of him as a man, for he was a doer of wonderful works, a teacher of such men as received the truth with pleasure."* Shakespeare pays a lowly reverence to Christ in passage after passage. Richter calls him "the holiest among the mighty, and the mightiest among the holy, who lifted with his pierced hand empires off their hinges and turned the stream of centuries out of its channel, and still governs the ages." Spinoza calls Christ "the symbol of divine wisdom." Kant and Jacobi hold Him up as "the symbol of ideal perfection;" and Schelling and Hegel as that of "the union of the divine and human." Strauss, the most learned infidel of modern times, in speaking of Christ, says that "he remains the highest model of religion within our thoughts, and that it is as absurd to think of religion without Christ as it is of poetry without regard to Homer and Shakespeare." Renan says: "Whatever will be the surprises of the future, Jesus will never be surpassed." Goethe says: "I esteem the Gospels to be thoroughly genuine, for there shines forth from them the reflected splendor of a sublimity, proceeding from the person of Jesus Christ, of so divine a kind as only the divine could ever have manifested on earth." "How petty are the books of the philosophers with all their pomp," exclaims Rosseau, the skeptic. "compared with the Gospels! Can it be that writings at once so sublime and so simple are the works of men? Can He, whose life they tell, be himself no more than a man? Is there anything in his character of the enthusiast or the ambitious sectary? What sweetness; what purity in his ways! What touching grace in his teachings! What a loftiness in his maxims! What profound wisdom in his words! What presence of mind, what delicacy and aptness in his replies! What an empire over his passions! Where is the man, where is the sage, who knows how to act, to suffer and to die without weakness and display? My friend, men do not invent like this; and the facts respecting Socrates, which no one doubts, are not so well attested as those about Jesus Christ. These Jews could never have struck this tone, or thought of this morality; and the Gospel has characteristics of truthfulness so grand, so striking, so perfectly inimitable, that their inventors would be even more wonderful than he whom they portray. If the life and death of

Socrates were those of a sage, the life and death of Jesus were those of a God." Thomas Carlyle says: "Jesus of Nazareth is our divinest symbol! Higher has the human thought not yet reached." Unitarian Channing acknowledges "that the character of Jesus Christ is wholly inexplicable on human principles." The first Napoleon, speaking of Christ, among other things said: "I see nothing here of man, near as I may approach, closely as I may examine. All remains above my comprehension. Great with a greatness that crushes me—it is in vain that I reflect. All remains unaccountable. I defy you to cite another life like that of Christ."

In Christ we have all that is lovely and attractive, true and good. The most perfect and excellent of all beings.

"Defects through nature's best productions run;
The saints have spots, and spots are on the sun."

But Christ was *altogether lovely*. All lights and no shades; all excellencies and no defects; all beauties and no blemishes.

We soon exhaust the most excellent characters of earth. But in the character of Christ there are depths, heights, lengths and breadths of loveliness that we can never exhaust.

"Nor earth, nor suns, nor seas, nor stars,
Nor heaven his full resemblance bears;
His beauties we can never trace
Till we behold him face to face.'

And after, in heaven, we shall have seen the King in his beauty as many millions of years as there are sands upon the sea-shore, there will still be in him an infinitude of undeveloped beauties to transport our expanding souls.

IV.

The Fullness of Time.

"When the fullness of time was come, God sent forth his Son."—*Gal.* iv: 4.

WHEN the fullness of time was come. The full time appointed by the Father. The exact period had arrived when all things were ready for His coming. But why did not the promised redemption immediately appear, in place of being delayed four thousand dark and gloomy years? Why did the world not at once receive the benefit of His incarnation and atonement?

This delay of redemption was in entire accord with the whole system of divine arrangements and interpositions in favor of men. On all subjects connected with human improvement and comfort the same question may be asked. Why were the medicines, the sciences, the arts and the inventions, which ward off disease, promote the intelligence, the happiness and the comfort of men, so long delayed? They were made known when the fullness of time had come; and so with redemption, Christ came at such a time when all the world would be most benefited by his coming.

It was a time when the prophets had centered in him, and when there was no question as to their fulfillment. And such an important event must be prophesied so far before the event as to make it impossible for men to say that it was mere guess-work.

The fitness of the time appears in the undeniable fact that there was at this time a general expectation throughout the world that a great prophet and deliverer would come, who should change the aspect of human affairs. The rumor seems to have advanced from the East, and to have reached the ears of the Roman Emperor. Josephus, Suetonius and Tacitus, mention that all the people at this very time believed that some one from Judea should obtain the empire of the world. There are many passages in heathen authors which prove that this expectation was prevalent at this time in the Oriental world, and especially in Judea. And the many instances of persons who appeared in Judea about this time, pretending to be the Messiah, and collected vast numbers of deluded Jews around them (facts repeatedly mentioned by the historians of that day), are additional proofs of this general persuasion. If we turn to the New Testament we find this state of things corroborated there by many incidental circumstances. The state of the public mind is indicated by Herod's anxiety upon hearing of the birth of a remarkable child in Bethlehem, and by the visit of the Eastern Magi. Still more illustrative is the thronging of the multitudes to John the Baptist upon his first appearance, and the message of the Pharisees and priests, to inquire if he were the Christ. "And all the people mused in their hearts if he were the Christ or not." Notice also the conversation of the Samaritan woman; her eagerness of the Messiah, as a prophet as well as a prince. Observe how the people pressed around Christ, demanding from heaven the sign which they expected of the Messiah. Observe how they caught at every appearance of extraordinary power; how, after his performance of a miracle, they were ready to take him by force and make him a king, and with what acclamations and royal honors the multitude accompanied him into Jerusalem. His humble condition alone restrained their enthusiasm. In a word, everything in profane history, and in the evangelical narratives, proves that the minds of the men of that age were wrought up to a high pitch of expectation, that the Great Prophet and King would soon come into the world.

It was needful that men should be prepared for salvation, and also that salvation should be prepared for men. Sin could not at once be abolished by a single effort of power, and salvation could not appear suddenly without due preparation. Like everything else that has a beginning, it must unfold itself in regular succession.

The world also had to be brought to see the need of a Saviour, and a fair opportunity had first to be given to men to try all the schemes of human redemption, and an experience of four thousand years taught the human race that salvation could not be obtained through man's own wisdom and strength. Not through the law of which Judaism was a proof; not through intellectual culture, science, art, eloquence or political power, of which the history of heathenism furnished the evidence. When Judaism was felt by the religious sense of the enlightened to be a type of a future and a better service, and when the cultured intellect of heathenism could not resist the conviction of its own emptiness and of its entire inability to satisfy the wants of man's moral nature, and when the various systems of religion devised had failed to arrest crime, to purify the heart, to elevate public morals, to support man in his trials, conduct him to the true God, and give him a well-grounded hope of immortality, man's extremity became God's opportunity. Then it was a proper time for God to send forth his Son and reveal a better system.

It was prophesied that Christ's kingdom was to be a

universal kingdom; hence there must be a political preparation. Rome then was the mistress of the world, and her conquering legions bore her banners from the Isles of Britain in the West to the Oriental cities in the East. In Europe, Asia and Africa there was but one vast empire, and the magnificent idea of a universal temporal kingdom, towards which the great heroes had hopelessly declined, was once more revived. The Greek language combined the whole world. The gates of the temple of Janus were closed for the second time during Roman history. The nations were waiting for a hero. Then the angel of history closed the old book and opened the new; and the name that is written on its title-page is —" Jesus Christ." He was the fountain from whence all subsequent history sprung. What an appropriate time for the coming of the Prince of Peace.

Now, to my mind, the very facts which show the fitness of the time for the introduction of Christianity are the very circumstances which show that the power of God must have been exerted in its origin and establishment.

Christ's universal expectation among the Jews led to his almost universal rejection. Their idea was a temporal deliverer, and his peaceable and unwarlike character disgusted them. His ignominious death was a stumbling-block. The fact that he was not saved by the power of God from the disgrace of crucifixion was everywhere regarded as a perfect answer to all his claims.

The Jews were odious to the Gentile world, and the consummation of Jewish prophecy to become the founder of a universal faith was too much for the wise men of Greece and Rome.

The corrupt morals of the pagan world were against the cordial reception of the Gospel. The apostles waged a tremendous war of extermination against their pompous sacrifices, their idol feasts, their dissolute worship and their favorite fights of gladiators, and at once, from the emperor on his throne down to his dissolute slaves, all were arrayed against the Gospel.

The intellectual refinement of the age was against the establishment of Christianity. The Greek language was spoken in all its purity, and elocution was everywhere cultivated. The apostles were publicans and fishermen, denominated by the ruling nations "barbarians." Such were the men who were to assault the high-fenced walls of Judaism, break the power of heathenism, though intrenched in the vices of the people, upheld by the power of the priesthood, and sanctioned by the traditions of memorial ages. Such were the men sent forth to go into the proud schools of philosophy, teach their teachers and bring out captives to the humble faith of the crucified Nazarene.

These then were the circumstances under which Christianity made such progress in the world, that in less than three hundred years a Christian emperor sat upon the throne of the Cæsars, and surpassed all that the philosophy and glory of Greece and Rome could boast. Nothing but facts which could not be denied, and the power of God exerted in the teachers of religion could have made this astonishing change in the world.

I see not only the fullness of the time when Jesus appeared, but from the unparalleled success of his religion, I am convinced that it was not only God who sent him forth, but that he sent forth his Son, whom to know aright is eternal life.

V.

The Right Vocation.

ONE of the most serious blunders young men frequently make is concerning their occupation or calling. The world is full of "square men in round holes, and round men in square holes." Many men have made shipwrecks of themselves and their prospects by rushing thoughtlessly into some business or profession for which nature never intended them. Dean Swift says:

> "Brutes find out where their talents lie ;
> A bear will not attempt to fly ;
> A foundered horse will not oft debate
> Before he tries a five-barred gate.
> A dog by instinct turns aside
> Who sees the ditch too deep and wide ;
> But man we find the only creature
> Who, led by folly, combats nature ;
> Who, when she loudly cries forbear !
> With obstinacy fixes there ;
> And where his genius least inclines
> Absurdly bends his whole designs."

The mischievous notion that a man to be respected must either be a preacher, doctor or lawyer has spoiled many a good carpenter, blacksmith or farmer. A shoemaker may put genius into his work, while a physician may only quack, a lawyer pettifog, and a preacher bore. It matters not what a man's vocation is, if pursued with an honorable spirit. Every man should do that to which he naturally and instinctively inclines. Take care before you decide. A change in a calling can seldom be made to advantage.

> "Honor and shame from no condition rise ;
> Act well your part; there all the honor lies."

VI.
The Sunday Question.

COMPARE the Sabbath-observing people with those who do not observe it; compare them as citizens, as business men; compare their influence in society, and then say whether the Sabbath with its means of grace is not useful. Let the comparison be fair and faithful. Do not select a few cases of rare inconsistency and hypocrisy in the churches, and set them over against rare virtue and good citizenship among those who, from education and habit, never attend the house of God. But look at the masses on both sides, and then decide which takes the wisest course: he who honors God's Sabbath, or he who lounges away the sacred hours in sleep and idleness, or seeks his own pleasure in travel and amusements, attends to his correspondence, etc., or visits his neighbors and friends to get a "a good square meal."

Ask yourself, ask history, ask matter of fact, what the Sabbath with its means of grace has done for the land in which you live. Compare your country, where the Sabbath is duly observed in every neighborhood, with those countries which rarely enjoy this blessing, where there are no Sabbath-schools, where preaching occurs only on great festival occasions, and where all are taught to look upon the holy day as a *holiday*. Sunday—*sin-day*. Blot out our churches from the map of our city, let teachers of religion and morals cease their works, and the people, instead of attending church, throng the streets and attend public places of amusement, gamble and drink, and train up their children to follow their unholy examples—what would be the state of society?

History most clearly proves that every nation and community has been prospered while it honored God's Sabbath, and that social order and the supremacy of the law have not been maintained where the Sabbath has been trampled on. Look abroad over the map of popular freedom in the world, and Switzerland, Scotland, England and the United States. the countries which best observe the Sabbath, constitute almost the entire map of safe popular government.

Some years ago, De Tochneville, the distinguished French statesman, was commissioned by his country for the purpose of studying the genius of our institutions. In reporting to the French Senate, he said : "I went at your bidding, and passed along their thoroughfares of trade. I ascended their mountains and went down their valleys. I visited their manufactories, their commercial markets, and emporiums of trade. I entered their judicial courts and legislative halls. But I sought everywhere in vain for the secret of their success. until I entered the church. It was there, as I listened to the soul-equalizing and soul-elevating principles of the Gospel of Christ, as they fell from Sabbath to Sabbath upon the masses of the people, that I learned why America was great and free, and why France was a slave."

De Montalembert, another French statesman, says: "Without a Sabbath, no worship, without worship, no religion, and without religion, no permanent freedom." Here we have the corner-stone of American liberties. There can be no permanent freedom without religion. and their can be no religion without worship, and there can be no worship without the Sabbath. Therefore, without the Sabbath there can be no permanent freedom. I believe that the security or disaster of American institutions depends upon the issue of the Sabbatic contest.

I believe also that the Sabbath question is a question of life and death in regard to Christianity. The enemies of religion tried the sword and the fagot. They could not destroy the Gospel. Imperial power found its arm too weak to contend with God. Argument, ridicule and sophistry were all in vain. Christianity rose with augmented power and more resplendent beauty. The last weapon the enemy seeks to employ to destroy Christianity and drive it from the land is to corrupt the Sabbath, make it a day of festivity, and make Christians feel that its sacred obligation has ceased. Voltaire truly said: "There is no hope of ever destroying the Christian religion, so long as the Sabbath is kept as a sacred day." Let us guard with holy jealousy that which is so essential to us as a people. It has been well said: "Take away the Sabbath, and you deprive man of his most humane and beneficent institution. Take away the Sabbath, and you destroy a mighty conservative force, and dry up a fountain from which the family, the church, and the state receive constant nourishment and support. Take away the Sabbath, and you shake the moral foundations of our national power and prosperity; our churches will be forsaken, our Sunday-schools emptied. our domestic devotions will languish, the fountains of public and private virtue will dry up, a flood of profanity, licentiousness and vice will inundate the land, labor will lose its reward, liberty be deprived of its pillar, self-government will prove a failure, and our republican institutions end in anarchy, confusion and despotism. Yes, the end of the Sabbath would be for the United States, the beginning of the reign of Mammon, Bacchus and Venus, and finally overwhelm us in temporal and eternal ruin." No, we cannot, we dare not—God Almighty helping us, we will not—give up the Sabbath.

VII.
High-Toned Scoundrelism.

THE refined and popular way of stealing in these days is to get into debt on a large scale, buy and borrow all you can, give your note, gracefully fail, and take advantage of the bankrupt laws—a new way of paying old debts. Strange, but true, a man will be treated kindly in proportion as his fall was severe. Smash on a small scale and the world will kick you; smash on a grand scale and the world will feel honored by being kicked by you. Go down for a few thousand and you are a rascal, and no one will trust you; go down for a hundred thousand, sweep away the livelihood of widows and orphans, poor girls, the aged and bedridden, and you will be pronounced unfortunate. The vulgar pickpocket is sent to jail. Steal a whole bank, and you are only a defaulter. "Fail! In the bright lexicon of youth there is no such word as fail." A man merely becomes embarrassed, and compromises with his creditors for twenty cents. What defaulters need is stripes. We want governors who cannot be moved by the pardon petitions of sentimental women and soft-headed men. Make hard times for the defaulters and there will be no more for the people. Let us not put a high premium upon crime by saying virtually to the young criminals of the country, what a safe thing it is to be a big thief. It is a disgrace to our public authorities that men notorious for financial criminality walk the streets of our city unwhipped of justice, and with a proud, defiant look, as much as to say: "Well, what are you going to do about it?" I tell you what I would like to do: brand upon their brows in shining letters the unmistakable word "*scoundrel!*" I would like all men to point at them the finger of scorn, and cry with a loud voice: "Stop thief!"

Let crime be given no quarter. Let the prison door be opened to the guilty, no matter what family connections he may have. High social standing only aggravates his guilt.

VIII.

The Tramp.

THE tramp is a confused workshop for the devil to tinker in. He is a nuisance in the world, and needs abatement for the public good. "If any man work not, neither should he eat," is St. Paul's bill of fare for the loafer. This extends to all who are able to work for a living, but will not do it. Work is an ordination of God, and greatly conducive to man's happiness. The commonest service, if it be right, is a real dignity.

I have one proposition for the tramp: on the side of him put healthy work, on the other put a whipping-post, and then let him take his choice.

If you help a man who prefers begging to work, and keep him from work and at begging, are you helping that man? Are you not injuring that man and the whole community? The tramp will come to you at times when it seems most heartless to refuse him. Don't believe the tales he tells. It is his business to invent pitiful and heart-rending tales. We even find children begging, early trained to roguery. Every thing they beg is converted into whisky. Ask them, where are your parents? "Dead." Yes; they are dead—*dead drunk*.

"If I could only get work," is the tramp's plea. Offer him work, and he is much obliged to you; but the hand is lame, the foot is sore, or he must dismiss his friend who is near by, so that he may not be kept waiting;

but it seems to take him all the day to dismiss his friend, as he never comes back. In other cases there are other excuses. The man who don't work, don't want to work; and a man who can work and won't work, ought to be compelled to work. To every man who comes within our city limits and says: " I would work if I could get work to do," should be given the reply of work to do in a place provided, to which he should be compelled to go by the strong arm of the law.

Let our churches and schools go to the root of the matter. Let men be taught that the world does not owe them a living. It was here first; it don't owe them anything. But every man owes the world work. We are born debtors to humanity. Idleness is a disgrace. It is not the mark of a "gentleman." The tramps of high society are in large measure responsible for the tramps of low society.

There are worthy poor, and they almost always never beg. They must be found. It is our duty to provide means for their relief. Let the work of beneficence be carried forth practically and judiciously, through our numerous organized and co-operative societies, covering all conceivable cases of need and suffering. To these contribute liberally. Refuse help to unknown parties, send them to these societies, and let each case be investigated; and the applicants that will not be helped by these societies, if in need, proclaim their unfitness for private beneficence.

There are unworthy poor. Good, friendly advice and work are worth more to them than money. They need moral culture. Our Christian duty is to impart it to them. " Bear ye one another's burdens, and so fulfill the law of Christ."

IX.
Intermarriage.

THE Bible forbids intermarriage with the world. The church is not to become mixed with the world by unholy alliances with the ungodly. Intermarriage so filled the antediluvian world with wickedness that the flood became a necessity. We read that the sons of God made love with the daughters of men. They expected by intermarriage to exert a predominating influence upon the wives, and of begetting and rearing up a godly seed, but the experiment proved a disastrous failure.

To-day the daughters of God are making love with the sons of men. Intermarriage with the world, in most cases, fills for mankind the cup of life with wormwood and gall. Fond lovers may call this a hard doctrine, and we may wound their susceptibilities, but nevertheless we are telling them the truth. The history of hundreds and thousands of those who have disregarded the divine law on this subject proves it true. Many a girl has had a happy connection with the church. It afforded her much satisfaction and real enjoyment. But she yoked herself with an unbeliever or a worldling. If she got to church she had to go alone, and her treatment was such if she went that life became miserable. And remember that bitter tears can never undo what you ought never to have done at first.

It is true, however, that a few religious women have brought their husbands to Christ, but many more have made shipwrecks of their own faith over the marriage altar.

The same may take place when a union is effected between two professors of religion, from two different religious denominations. The husband or the wife being a miserable bigot, knows of no religion but that of his or her own sect. He knows no church but *his* church; she knows no church but *her* church. At length the children become the subjects of dispute and ill-will. The husband authoritatively demands them to go with him— the mother claims her share. Harmony between husband and wife is destroyed—the family is thrown into confusion and strife. In such a case there is only one way of escape, and that is, to attend a church like this, where Christianity is not preached as a creed, but as the spirit of Christ living in our lives.

Husband and wife are said to be "one flesh;" but there is a great difference between a fleshly union, and a union of heart and spirit. Is marriage a Scriptural union, if the one be an infidel or a worldling, and the other a believer and a doer of the word? or if the religious beliefs are diametrically opposed to each other? It has been truly said: "Like oil and water cast into one vessel, they may be thrown together under one roof, but *life communion*, such as the marriage relation is designed to afford, they can never have." You know well that I have no hostile feelings towards those whose religious views are other than mine. I have spoken with distinctness because of a sincere desire to guard your most sacred interests, and secure to you, young ladies and gentlemen, that happiness without which life will be charmless and joyless. I therefore unhesitatingly express the opinion that marriages between persons who do not tread in the same religious path are wholly unadvisable—nay, wrong, for they tend to invite a future teeming with shadows, clouds and darkness.

X.

Good Housekeeping.

A GOOD wife must be a good housekeeper. No matter what a girl's accomplishments may be, her education is incomplete if she has not some knowledge in the sciences of *bake-ology, boil-ology, cook-ology, stitch-ology* and *mend-ology*. All experience and observation show that good housekeeping is one of the most essential elements of happiness in the household. Even if a girl should never be required to do the work herself, she ought to know whether the work is done in the proper manner or not.

> "Give me the fair one in city or country,
> Whose home and its duties are dear to her heart."

Then, too, do not forget that the rich of to-day are very often to-morrow's poor. Crœsus, whose name is a synonym for great wealth, was himself taken captive, stripped of all his treasures, and in his old age supported by the charity of Cyrus.

The greatest defect in our social system is the aimless way in which girls are brought up. Nine-tenths of them are prepared in neither body nor mind for the lofty duties and serious responsibilities which marriage implies, and marriage, in consequence, has been brought down to a low, sensual plane. Let our girls be brought up to have their regular daily domestic duties, let idleness be forbidden them, and let every woman be clothed with the dignity of a useful life. The great secret of domestic tranquillity lies in a good, square meal. Meredith says :

"We may live without poetry, music and art ;
We may live without conscience; we may live without heart;
We may live without friends ; we may live without books,
But civilized man cannot live without cooks.
He may live without books; what is knowledge but grieving?
He may live without hope ; what is hope but deceiving?
He may live without love ; what is passion but repining ?
But where is the man that can live without dining?"

With Dr. Holland we believe that there is but one cure for many of our social evils, and that is "universal housekeeping." No hotel or boarding house, however pleasant, can supply the want created by an instinctive heart-longing for some place, "be it ever so lowly," which can be called—*our home.*

"A charm from the skies seems to hallow us there,
Which, seek through the world, is ne'er met with elsewhere."

XI.
Unequally Yoked Together.

VID says: "If you wish to marry suitably, marry your equal." If possible marry a man who is in some way your superior. Your standing in society will be determined by his. If you marry your inferior you wrong yourself, your family and your whole life. As Shakespeare says:

"'Tis meet that noble minds
Keep ever with their likes."

True are the words of Tennyson in Locksley Hall of every woman who marries her inferior:

" Thou shalt lower to his level day by day,
What is fine within thee growing coarse to sympathize with clay.
As the husband is, the wife is; thou art mated with a clown,
And the grossness of his nature will have power to drag thee down.
He will hold thee when his passion shall have spent its novel force,
Something better than his dog, a little dearer than his horse."

Now and then a woman of great force of character may lift her husband upward, but she accepts such a labor at the risk of her own higher life. Do not misunderstand me. I do not say that you shall marry for ambition; This is Mrs. Carlyle's experience. She said: "I married for ambition; Carlyle has exceeded all that my wildest hopes ever imagined of him, and I am miserable." Yet there is no great danger marrying geniuses, as the supply is very limited. Many men think themselves geniuses, and try to make the female sex believe that they are not made of common clay, and that the girl who gets them will be blessed. From such a blessing I would have you adopt the Episcopalian prayer: "*Good Lord deliver us.*"

XII.
Beauty.

BEAUTY is said to be only skin deep. Sometimes it is no deeper than the powder and the paint.

> " 'Tis not the fairest form that holds
> The mildest, purest form within;
> 'Tis not the richest plant that holds
> The sweetest fragrance in."

Many a fair face hides a foul heart. A woman's worth is to be estimated by the real goodness of her heart, the greatness of her soul, the purity of her character, the sweetness of her disposition and well-balanced temper. A woman with these qualities, be she ever so plain, or even homely, makes the best of wives and truest of mothers. She will have a higher purpose in living than fluttering around dry-goods and millinery stores, like a butterfly around a gaudy flower, ever on the lookout for the latest style. A good many women have the *delirium trimmins.*

To love dress is not to be the slave of fashion. Elegance fits you. I believe that the love of beauty and refinement belongs to you. Nor am I opposed to pleasure and gayety. But this is not the only object of your creation. Don't give gayety and style your first thought, your best time, and all your money. I would have you be troubled more by a neglected duty than an unfashionable bonnet. Consult the Bible oftener than *Harper's Bazar,* and follow the Saviour more closely than Madame Demorest!

The most pitiable creatures I ever saw were the husbands of "professional beauties." They all believe with Socrates, that beauty is "a short-lived tyranny;" and with Theophrastus, "a silent cheat." What you want, young man, in a wife, is not a toy to play with, a doll to be dressed, an ornament to exhibit, but a "helpmeet," not simply a help-cat.

> "Woe to him who weds for life
> Some female cipher called a *wife;*
> Who, destitute of brains or heart,
> Leaves him not free to act his part;
> A torture on the tyrant's plan,
> Which chains a carcass to a *man!*
> Go wed a Tartar for your bride,
> Or yoke Xanthippe to your side;
> But let not Hymen's holy chain
> Bind you to some one fair but vain,
> Who, next to dress, loves you best,
> And has no soul to make you blest!
> Far better is *acidity*
> Than flat, stale insipidity;
> And such a female is no *woman*—
> Her husband must be more than human."

XIII.
"A Friend in Need is a Friend Indeed."

LORD BACON says: "To be without friends, is to find the world a wilderness." A Portuguese proverb says: "There is no living without friends." Robinson Crusoe might glory on his lonely island in being monarch of all he surveyed, but he was heartily glad when he got the company of the man Friday. It is only a mean man that can be contented alone. God intended us for society. A trusty friend is one of earth's greatest blessings.

Beware, as for your life, of the friendships you form. Alas! for the dire contagion of evil friendships! Be scrupulous as to whom you admit to your confidence and affections. Washington was wont to say: "Be courteous to all, intimate with few, and let those few be well tried before you give them your confidence." Aim high. Get into the best society possible. Slight no man for poverty, nor esteem any man for his wealth.

Stick to your friend. He can never have any true friends who is often changing them. To part with a tried friend, without any great provocation, is unreasonable levity.

Bring your friend to a proper understanding of himself. Persuade him from his follies. "Rebuke a wise man," says Solomon, "and he will love thee." Phocion said truly to Antipater: "I cannot be both your friend and flatterer."

"A FRIEND IN NEED IS A FRIEND INDEED." 49

True friendship cannot exist between bad men. The degree of their privacy to each other's wickedness will be the measure of their dislike and distrust.

True friendship is tested in the hour of adversity. No lack of friends when all goes prosperously with you; but that is not the time to form the estimate of the friendship. Wait until you are in trouble, and many a professed friend will be shy of you, and give you the dead cut. It is remarkable how few the friendships are that bear the strain of altered circumstances and remain true as the needle to the pole. *"A friend in need is a friend indeed."*

Many people expect too much from their friends. Their friends must do everything for them; give them flaming testimonials of character; lend them no end of money; become their sureties for a loan, and get them out of every scrape into which their improvidence gets them. Hence, we quite agree with that old saying: "Friends, like fiddle-strings, must not be screwed too tight."

Friendships are often productive of mischief because they are not governed by wisdom and prudence. Many a man clings to his friends like the ivy to the oak for support, so that his energies are never called out, and his talents are never brought into exercise. Stand on your own legs. Be independent. You are better off without any friends than with such as are prepared to help you whenever you get into trouble; for with such friends you will always be getting into trouble, and will never learn how to get yourself out of it. The young man who begins with crutches the battle of life, generally ends on crutches.

He is our best friend who is a friend to our soul. Give a wide berth to the sneering skeptic. Have for your bosom friends men who will "strengthen your hand in God," who will foster your piety, and make you wiser, better and holier men.

In closing, we wish to introduce you to a Friend who will prove to you the kindest and truest friend you ever had. "He sticketh closer than a brother." For friend and brother are by no means equivalent. A man's worst foes are frequently those of his own household. "Many kinsfolk, few friends."

In Christ alone our proverb finds its verification. Jesus is for every man "a friend in need," and therefore "a friend indeed."

> "One there is above all others
> Well deserves the name of Friend;
> His is love beyond a brother's,
> Lasting, true, and knows no end."

XIV.

Revenge.

BYRON says: "Sweet is revenge." But we rather agree with Milton:

"Revenge, at first though sweet,
Bitter, ere long, back on itself recoils."

Juvenal says: "Revenge is only the pleasure of a little, weak and narrow mind." Lord Karnes truly says: "The indulgence of revenge tends to make men more savage and cruel." The dog believes that revenge is sweet, and, with almost human tenacity, cherishes ideas of revenge. He neither forgives nor forgets. Revenge is not *manhood;* it is rather *doghood.* When you are tempted to give the cutting or hasty answer, check yourself with the question: "Is this the reply my Saviour would have given?" If your fellow-men should prove unkind, inconsiderate and ungrateful, be it yours to refer the cause to God. *Revenge!* No such word should have a place in the Christian's vocabulary. *Revenge!* If I cherish such a feeling towards my brother, how can I meet that brother in heaven? "But ye have not so learned in Christ." Christ did not answer cutting taunts and meet unmerited wrong. "Overcome evil with good." "Who, when he was reviled, reviled not again." "Let this mind be in you which was also in Christ Jesus."

XV.
Grumblers.

EVERYTHING goes wrong with some people because they make it. They never have any pleasure because they never get ready to enjoy it. Everything is out of humor and so are the people. Something is wrong all the time, and the wrong is with them. Their lot is harder than falls to other mortals; their home is the worst of anybody's; they have more trouble than anybody else; they are never so happy as when they grumble; and, if everything worked to their satisfaction, they would still grumble because there was nothing for them to grumble about. The grumbler is a violator of God's law, and a sinner against the peace and harmony of society. While we are perfectly willing the grumbler should go to heaven at death, everybody is heartily glad to get rid of him on earth.

Don't torment yourselves with borrowed troubles. Don't wait for happiness. Go to work and make it. Adopt the true philosophy of life. Take things as they come. Look at the bright side. If there is no bright side, brush up one of the dark ones. Don't hang down your heads or lips. "Nothing so bad but it might have been worse." "It is a long lane that has no turning." "'Tis always morning somewhere in the world." "Every cloud has a silver lining." "The darkest hour of the night is that which precedes the dawn." Form the habit of thinking how much there is to cheer you, even when there may be much to depress. A poor widow, not having bed-clothes to shelter her boy from the snow which was blown through the cracks of her miserable ιovel, used to cover him with boards. One night he said to her smilingly and contentedly: "Ma, what do poor folks do these cold nights that haven't any boards to put on their children?" A poor widow living in a house open to snow in winter, and who could have no fire when the wind blew, exclaimed: "How favored I am! For when it is coldest and the wind does not blow, I can have a fire." When rheumatism had disabled one of her feet, she exclaimed again: "How favored I am! I once lost use of both my feet." Thus, in every calamity she saw some especial mercy. "How dismal you look," said a bucket to his companion as they were going to the well, "Ah!" replied the other, "I was reflecting on the uselessness of our being filled: for let us go away ever so full, we always come back empty." "Dear me! How strange to look at it in that way," said the other bucket. "Now I enjoy the thought that however *empty* we come, we always go away *full*. Only look at it in that light and you will be as cheerful as I am."

Solon being asked by Crœsus who in the world was happier than himself, answered: "Tellus, who, though he was poor, was a good man and content with what he had, and died at a good old age." What a glorious world this would be if all its inhabitants could say with Shakespeare's shepherd: "Sir, I am a true laborer. I earn what I wear; owe no man hate; envy no man happiness; glad of other men's good; contented with my farm." Cultivate what is warm and genial, not the cold and the repulsive, the sullen and the morose. Smile and all nature will smile with you; the air will seem more balmy, the sky more clear, the grass will have a brighter green, the trees a richer foliage, the flowers a more fragrant smell, the birds will sing more sweetly, and the sun, moon and stars will appear more beautiful.

XVI.
Gossipers.

BUSINESS is business, but the best kind of business is to mind your own business, and the reason why those people succeed so well who mind their own business is because there is so little competition. Woman generally gets the credit for the gossiping business. It is said that when the Lord made man he gave him ten measures of speech, and that the woman ran away with nine of them. The Chinese say that a woman's sword is her tongue and she never lets it rest. Many a woman's tongue is like an express train running along at the rate of forty miles an hour, pouring out its rain of sparks on every side and setting everything on fire. But justice compels me to say that the men are just as bad blabs as the women. Indeed, many women have gone out of the gossiping business, and babbling, tattling, sly-whispering, and impertinent, meddling men have succeeded them, and are trespassing constantly on the community with their tongues.

There is a sad propensity in our fallen nature to listen to the gossips and scandal-mongers. Without any intention of doing injury to a neighbor, a careless remark may be seized by a babbler, and, as a snow-ball grows by rolling it, so does a story by telling: it passes through the babbling tribe, growing larger and larger, and darker and darker, and by the time it has rolled through Babbletown, it has assumed the magnitude and blackness of base slander.

Especially is this true of the fair sex. An injurious rumor against a person of unblemished character, originating with some gossip, once attached to a person's name, will remain beside it in a blemish and doubt forever. Many a woman has withered and melted like snow in the spring, shedding burning tears of sadness over man's unkindness, and woman's inhumanity to woman, which

"Has made countless thousands mourn."

Among many species of animals, if one of their number is wounded and falls, he is at once torn to pieces by his fellows. Traces of this animal cruelty are seen in men to-day, but especially in women. Let a woman fall from virtue, and nine-tenths of her sisters will turn and tear her to pieces, and the next day the man who robbed her of her virtue, broke her father's and her mother's hearts, and drove her to the street, will be smiled on and almost congratulated on his success. The cruelty of woman to woman is perfectly wolfish. Shame, oh, shame! Reverse the action: loathing for the unrepentant wretch who accomplished her ruin, and tenderness for the wounded sister.

Believe but half the ill and credit twice the good said of your neighbor. If you can say nothing good of him, say nothing at all. Deal tenderly with the absent. Beecher says: "When the absent are spoken of, some will speak gold of them, some silver, some iron, some lead, and some always speak dirt, for they have a natural attraction toward what is evil, and think it shows penetration in them. As a cat watching for mice does not look up, though an elephant goes by, so they are so busy mousing for defects that they let great excellencies pass them unnoticed. I will not say that it is not *Christian* to make beads of others, and tell them over every day. I say it is *infernal*. If you want to know how the devil feels, *you do know* if you are such a one."

Fault-finders are always small souled. The ignorant laugh, and ridicule, and criticise. True worth never exults in the faults of others. "Faults are always thick where love is thin." "A white cow is all black if your eyes choose to make it so."

When an eminent painter was requested to paint Alexander the Great, so as to give a perfect likeness of him, he felt a difficulty. Alexander in his wars had been struck by a sword, and across his forehead was an immense scar. The painter said: "If I retain the scar, it will be an offense to the admirers of the monarch, and if I omit it, it will fail to be a perfect likeness. What shall I do?" He hit upon a happy expedient, he represented the Emperor leaning on his elbow, with his forefinger upon his brow, accidentally, as it seemed, covering the scar on his forehead. So let us study to paint each other with the finger of charity upon the scar of a brother or a sister, hiding the ugly mark, and revealing only the beautiful, the true and the good.

XVII.
Is Christianity Failing?

THE noisy infidels have for over three centuries said: "Christianity is virtually extinct, and now we are to have a new order of things." But, for some reason or other, Christianity does not die, and the world moves forward in much the same way.

What is infidelity? A murderous hand reaching up through the smoke of the pit, to smite and blast, to curse and destroy, to drag down bodies and souls of immortal men into the prison-house of woe. Infidelity is nothing new. It has left a blasted fire-track, stretching from the very walls of heaven, across fair Eden, down the long ages of time into the blackness of eternal darkness. What has infidelity done for the world? Where are the testimonies of the work it has wrought? Where are its temples! Where are its schools and colleges? Where are its hospitals? Where are its organized societies of benevolence? What has it benefited society? What has it done for the elevation and purity of public morals? What science or art has it originated? How many slaves has it liberated? How many inebriates has it reclaimed? How many fallen women has it restored? When hot war tramped the land with iron heel, what did infidelity do for the relief of the wounded and dying soldier-boy? What has it done to pioneer new countries for civilization? Where did it ever create a single virtue? What life has it ever assisted to higher holiness? What death has it ever cheered? None, none! Nor can it. Its nature forbids hope. It only bewilders, and confuses, and perplexes, and tortures, and damns. But it has an object. It is to destroy. It raves and foams against God, and the Bible, and the Sabbath, and the family, and the church, and the state. It would open wide the flood-gates of vice, plunge the world into the grave of despair, and consign humanity to the dungeons of the damned. We have nothing to hope from infidelity, but everything to dread.

There was one nation, and only one, that ever tried this system of infidelity—one nation that succeeded in persuading the people that they would die like brutes, and they began to live like brutes. France decreed in national convention that there was no God and death an eternal sleep. The Sabbath was abolished, churches were turned into temples of reason, the Bible was dragged along the streets by way of derision and contempt. Infidelity then reigned and frightful was its reign. Its crown was terror, its throne the guillotine, its sceptre the battle-axe, its palace yard a field of blood, and its royal robes dripped with human gore. Gutters were filled with the torn shreds of human flesh. Property was confiscated. The morning breeze and evening wind bore across the vine-clad hills of France the cries of suffering and the shrieks of terror. And to save the metropolis and the kingdom from utter desolation, the infidel authorities had to institute the Sabbath and public worship.

Infidelity is a failure—an inglorious failure. The history of the past proves that the human mind can not be satisfied with what the Germans very properly denominate *Wurst-Philosophie*. The most hostile theories against Christianity have been speedily abandoned, and the best thought of the age bows reverently to the claims of Christianity.

The enemies of religion have striven among themselves and fiercely demolished one another. The theory of Paulus was soon displaced by that of critical Strauss. The theory of Strauss was in turn destroyed by that of the æsthetic Renan. The theory of Renan has fallen to pieces of its own inconsistencies. Baur, Hilgenfeld and Schwegler, like sappers and miners with pick-axe and powder, went forth to subvert Christianity, but they have only disclosed the Gibraltar strength of her foundations. Voltaire said he lived in the twilight of Christianity. He told the truth, although he meant a lie. He did live in its twilight, but not as he meant to say, the twilight of the evening; it was the twilight before the morning. Voltaire and his theories have sunk into the night of the past. Christianity lives in the twilight of the present. He, too, boasted that with one hand he would overthrow the fabric of Christianity, which required the hands of twelve apostles to build up, and to-day the press which he employed to print his blasphemies is used in printing the Bible, and the house in which he lived is packed with Bibles from garret to cellar as a depot for the Bible Society. Gibbon labored earnestly to overthrow Christianity, yet to-day Gibbon's hotel at Lake Leman contains a room where Bibles are sold. Chesterfield's parlor, formerly an infidel club-room, echoing with profanity and raillery at the Christian religion, is now a vestry where the groans and prayers of the penitent go up to God. Tom Paine thought he had demolished the Bible, but after he had crawled desparingly into a drunkard's grave in 1809, the book took such a leap that since that time more than twenty times as many Bibles have been made and scattered through the world as were ever made before since the creation of man. A few years ago a man traveled around the country showing up "The Mistakes of Moses," at about five hundred dollars a night. I would not give ten cents to hear the infidel on the mistakes of Moses, but I would give one hundred dollars to hear Moses on the mistakes of the infidel. It would be interesting to hear a military leader and legislator like Moses, who, after he was eighty years old, commanded for forty years an army of six hundred thousand men, emancipating, organizing and giving laws to a nation which has maintained its existence for more than thirty centuries, give his candid opinion concerning the "mistakes" of a "colonel" of cavalry, whose military career is said to have included one single engagement, in which "he was chased into a hog yard and surrendered to a boy of sixteen, after which he heroically resigned his commission in the face of the enemy," subsequently turning his attention to managing a swindling whisky ring, discussing theology, blaspheming God, setting up men of straw and knocking them down, criticising dead men and dead issues, and defending Star Route thieves for a cattle *rancho* in New Mexico.

Infidelity has had its era. A little over a century ago England was under the dominion of infidelity. But a reaction came, and to-day Gladstone, the greatest living Englishman, is an earnest teacher in the Sunday-school, and the Bible the text-book of every British youth. At the close of the last century, and far into our own, infidelity was predominant in Germany; but in our day not only are devout believers the masters of her mind, but the presses of England and America teem with the products of her faith.

Christianity is far from being a creed outworn. Christianity and civilization are identical. The one cannot be carried forward without the other. Wherever go the swift ships, wherever stretch the electric wires or the iron rails, there goes the cross, the grand magnetic centre of the creation of God. Church bells are ringing everywhere, grand cathedrals are arising on every shore and plain; on wilds and continents unknown Christ is setting up his throne. Christianity is making inroads everywhere, and is spreading most in the most advanced and cultured nations. This is not the case with Mohammedanism, Buddhism, Confucianism and Brahmanism. They burrow among the superstitious and uncultured. China, the most populous and wealthy of all heathen countries, compelled by the force of circumstances to open its doors to the outside world, has been penetrated by missionary pioneers to Thibet on the west and Burma on the south, and fully one-half of its provinces from Hong Kong and Canton as far as Pekin have been occupied by a chain of missions which take in the principal cities of the Empire. Japan, which in its thirst for progress and improvement has opened the way for the preaching of the Gospel, already rejoices in the organization of scores of evangelical churches. In the Mohammedan countries, from the Balkan Mountains on the north to Bagdad on the south, from Egypt on the west to Persia on the east, central points in the most prominent cities have been established for the evangelization of the Moslem population.

All the great religions are going down, while the glad tidings proclaimed to the shepherds on Judea's plains are spread abroad as never before. With the Bible translated into more than three hundred different languages and dialects, with missionary stations planted on every shore, with dark continents opened for the heralds of salvation, with long isolated nations unbarring their gates and flinging open wide their moss-grown portals, with the isles of the sea stretching out their hands to God, with servants and hand-maidens, on whom the Spirit of God has been poured out, flying as on the wings of the wind to bear the message of salvation to a lost world, with all the appliances of modern science and the activities of modern enterprise and intellect, the way is sure for the Gospel of Christ to reach the very ends of the earth.

Christianity is on the eve of fresh victories. She is just raising herself. Oh! I see her. There is beauty on her brow, there is lustre in her eye, there is glory on her cheek. I see her stepping on the mountains, passing over the plains; I see her fair white hand, with nail-scars and blood-drops on it, stretching down through the clouds of wrath, distributing blessings on the sons of men, lifting helpless sinners from bondage and misery into liberty and joy, and placing them high above the seats of angels and archangels.

The church is the only institution left standing in the world which carries the mind back to the times when the smoke of sacrifice rose from the Pantheon, and when camelopards and tigers bounded in the Flavian amphitheatre. The Christian church was great and respected before the Saxon had set foot on Great Britain—before the Frank had passed the Rhine—when Grecian eloquence still flourished at Antioch; and she still exists, divinely beautiful, divinely wise, divinely beneficent; she still lives with an immortal life, radiant with an imperishable beauty, surrounded by the wrecks of a thousand kingdoms and empires that have been swept away, while she is yet young. The dew of youth is yet upon her, and she comes as an angel down to the lowest depths of the fall, building ascending steps of deliverance that reach the very throne of God, and link heaven and earth together. Over against 82,000 ministers, 886,000 Sunday-school teachers and more than 18,000,000 communicants in this country, there is to-day but one popular infidel lecturer, and he no more impedes the progress of the church than a snow-flake would a lightning express train. His attack upon the church is fully as laughable as the attack of a fly upon a bumble-bee, a weasel upon a lion, or a canary bird upon an eagle. He might as well endeavor to turn back the flowing tide with a wisp of straw, outroar a hurricane with a tin whistle, hold the wind in his fist, suspend the succession of the seasons by his nod, or extinguish the light of the sun with a veil. Foolish man! He is but plowing the air, striking with a straw, writing on the surface of the water, and seeking figs where only brambles grow.

A certain circuit judge was always sure of meeting some cutting or sneering remarks from a self-conceited lawyer when he came to a certain town in his rounds. This was repeated one day at dinner, when a gentleman present said: "Judge, why don't you squelch that fellow?" The judge, dropping his knife and fork, and placing his chin upon his hands and his elbows on the table, remarked: "Up in our town a widow had a dog that, whenever the moon shone, went upon the steps and barked, and barked away at it all night." Stopping short he quietly resumed eating. After waiting some time it was asked: "Well, Judge, what of the dog and the moon?" "*Oh! the dog died and the moon keeps on shining,*" he said. So all the Injuresouls will die, and Christianity will shine on.

The church is established on the top of the mountain, and all the nations are flowing unto it. The times are full of promise. Everything is hopeful. The liberality of Christians is greater than ever. The Bible is read by a larger proportion of the world's people than in any previous age. When the revised version of the New Testament was placed in market, one publishing house in New York sold 250,000 copies before three o'clock in the afternoon. The printing press sends forth 2400 Bibles every day. Each Lord's Day the Bible is studied by over 9,000,000 children in the Sunday-schools of our land alone. In the year 1500 the number of Christians was 100,000,000; at the beginning of the present century the number was 200,000,000, but now the number is over 450,000,000. Christianity in the last eighty-six years gained more than in 1800 years previous. From 1850 to 1880 the increase of population in our land was 116 per cent.; of communicants in the same period, 184 per cent. Thus it is evident that the ratio of communicants has exceeded that of the population 68 per cent.

By the multiplied agencies of church-work over 6000 are converted per day—a Pentecost every twelve hours. The Methodist Church in this country alone is building two churches a day. In seven decades the Christians of America contributed voluntarily $129,905,000 for missions. The amounts raised for ministers' salaries, for the running expenses of 115,610 churches, for repairs, for new churches, for the benevolences, colleges, etc., etc., we dare not undertake to compute. The aggregate must be an enormous sum. Now, would a religion be supported with such amazing generosity if the people did not believe in it, and if it were dying out?

Church-going, if not more popular, is more respectable to-day than ever. Let a stranger come into any community. The first question is: "Where do you go to church?" Where is there a community in the United States where the most intelligent and respectable people do not attend and support the church? Seven-eighths of the members of the American Association for the Advancement of Science are either church members or church attendants. Never in the history of American politics were so many of the leading statesmen church members. In 1745 only four or five students in Yale College were church members; William and Mary's College was a hot-bed of infidelity. In Bowdoin only one student dared to avow himself a Christian. How is it to-day? Take the oldest of American universities. Dr. Dorchester, in his "Problem of Religious Progress," says: "Inquiries extending through 1400 graduates of Harvard within the last ten years show only two skeptics, and never before were there so many evangelical church members among the students of that institution." The same is true of Yale. Dr. McCosh testifies that since his connection with Princeton over 1200 young men have graduated; of that number four left the institution confirmed infidels. Since graduation even these four have considered the grounds of their unbelief and returned to the stand of Christianity.

The pulpit is aided by thousands of magazines and great numbers of periodicals of various kinds. Journalism has grown so that now no respectable daily newspaper is without its religious news. No danger of Christianity failing. Dispel all fear.

Christianity is safe. It is the living faith of the world's best civilization. It has associated itself with the best and most enduring literature, the noblest forms of art, the broadest system of education, the most liberal systems of government, the most progressive theories of human development, the purest social state, the most practical and successful endeavors for the amelioration of human suffering and the extension of human happiness, and in fine with every element of dignity, prosperity and power among the nations of the earth. The name Christian, given a few humble followers of Christ at Antioch eighteen hundred and twenty-six years ago as a term of reproach, is now blazoned on the banners of the greatest kingdoms of the earth, and borne with pride by the world's best civilization.

Its grand facts are constellated in eternal beauty, and in the dispensation of the fullness of the spirit of the Almighty God, the knowledge of the Lord shall cover the earth as the waters cover the sea, and Jesus shall reign from sea to sea, and from the rivers unto the ends of the earth. Kings shall become nursing fathers and queens nursing mothers to the church of the living God, and gospel truth and gospel righteousness shall become the law of the nations.

Hope thou in God. The power is his. The grace is his. The mighty attraction of the cross shall yet draw men to the crucified, and Jesus shall see the travail of his soul and be satisfied.

Amid all the world's overturnings and uncertainties, Christianity, like the imperial oak whose roots strike deep and wide, and whose summit stretches towards the heavens, towers aloft in its own native majesty, and proudly bids defiance to every assault. Thick and hot as the flames of persecution gather around it and threaten it, like the bush of Horeb, it remains entire amid all the flames. He who planted it hath said: "The gates of hell shall not prevail against it." Thrones may fall, empires perish, confederations dissolve, nations vanish, and

> "The proudest works of Genius shall decay,
> And Reason's brightest lustre fade away;
> The sophists' art, the poet's boldest flight,
> Shall sink in darkness and conclude in night;"

but the church, triumphant over time, shall stand and its branches wave in glory in the sky when the world itself shall be no more. It can no more perish than God himself can die; for he is in it, and has linked it to his own immortality.

"Alleluia! for Lord God Omnipotent reigneth."

XVIII.
Wanted—A Man.

IT should be the highest ambition of every man to possess true manhood. And what is so sublime a thing as a man—a real man—a true man! To be a man—a genuine man—is everything. It is to be the best thing beneath the skies. To be a man is something more than to live to be twenty-one years of age—something more than to grow to the physical stature of man.

Three thousand years ago the prophet Jeremiah said: "Run ye to and fro through the streets of Jerusalem, and see now, and know, and seek in the broad places thereof if ye can find a man." But Jeremiah was "the weeping prophet." Philosophers in all ages have complained that human creatures are plentiful, but men are scarce. But philosophers made their ideal too high, their conception of what man ought to be too lofty. I have no sympathy with the cynic of whom history informs us, that, being ordered to summon the good men of the city before the Roman censor, proceeded immediately to the graveyard, called to the dead below, saying he knew not where to find a good man alive; or that gloomy sage, that prince of grumblers, Thomas Carlyle, who described the population of his country as consisting of so many millions, "mostly fools," and who could speak in praise of no one but himself and Mrs. Carlyle, the latter deserving all the praise she got for enduring him so long. When any one complains, as the famous Diogenes did, that he has to hunt the streets with candles at noonday to find an honest man, we are apt to think that his nearest neighbor would have quite as much difficulty as himself in making the discovery. If you think there is not a true man living, you had better, for appearance, put off saying it until you are dead yourself.

In looking for a man, look for a man with a conscience—a man who, like Longfellow's honest blacksmith, can " look the whole world in the face, and fear not any man." Look for a being that has a heart. A warm, loving nature is true manliness. In looking for a man, look for a magnanimous man; a broad mind, that not only observes what passes in the limited range of its own sphere, but is not afraid to look abroad; is far-sighted and not afraid of excellence in others.

In your search for " a man," look for a being that has a soul—the capability of solemn thought.

> " A little nonsense now and then
> Is relished by the best of men."

But some men are so given to levity that they are incapable of a serious thought. Thousands to-day worship Bacchus and Venus. Their hearts are set on having " a good time." Others apply themselves so intensely to their business, that they find pleasure only in worshiping the mighty dollar. The man who so inordinately loves money for its own sake, and becomes insensible to all refined enjoyments, after awhile ceases to be a man. Out of the gold which the woman brought to Aaron he made a golden calf. That operation is being repeated over and over again every day. Many a man has gathered so much gold together that instead of making a man of him it made him a golden calf. Money does not make the man. Goldsmith hints this when he says:

> "Ill fares the land, to hastening ills a prey,
> When wealth accumulates and men decay."

"How much, then, is a man better than a sheep" if, as Tennyson says, "he nourishes a blind life within the brain"—blind to God and immortality? Striking and grand are these lines Burns sent to an intimate friend:

> "The voice of nature loudly cries—
> And many a message from the skies—
> That something in us never dies:
> That in this frail, uncertain state,
> Hang matters of eternal weight;
> That future life, in worlds unknown,
> Must take its hue from this alone;
> Whether as heavenly glory bright,
> Or dark as misery's woeful night.
> Since then, my honored first of friends,
> On this poor being all depends,
> Let us the important NOW employ,
> And live as those who never die."

Faith in Jesus Christ makes manly men. "By faith," says St. Peter, "we become partakers of the divine nature." Then only will we be men in the highest sense. Would you be men? Imitate Christ. He is our model—a model containing all the elements of true manhood: a model of sympathy and love; a model of purity and uprightness. *Christ-men* are wanted.

XIX.
Crimes and Criminals.

THE highest interests of society demand that every criminal be speedily punished to the full extent of the law. Too many criminal matters are "fixed up," while the interests of society are fixed down. All over this country society realizes the imperative need of a more speedy and effective administration of the criminal law—a more certain and expeditious execution of justice, which would send terror to the hearts of the evil-doers. If every criminal should be given to understand that he would be severely punished immediately after the committal of the crime, crime would walk more slowly among us.

The jury-box must be regenerated, purified, and placed on a higher pedestal. Changes are needed which will assure the public that intelligence, uprightness, good moral character, and respectable common sense are in the jury-box. I believe that the jury system is immovably imbedded in the structure and character of our civilization, but it does not yield satisfactory results as an agency in the administration of justice. Trial by jury has been degraded to a contemptible farce in many parts of our country. Every blockhead, every ignoramus and every corrupt knave that is permitted to vote can discharge the functions of a juror. It is a common and true saying in this country, that ignorance is the best jury qualification, and intelligence the greatest disqualification. We need a change in our law, so that only intelligent and sensible men can serve as jurors. To bring this about we must educate and agitate; and we must have men who are willing to serve their country in the capacity of jurors: and to this end we need a law that will allow respectable pay, so that respectable men can be secured.

Criminal lawyers are in a large measure to blame for the large number of crimes and criminals. When a man has committed a crime, he weighs his chances to escape punishment by the amount of money he is able to pay a lawyer for his defense. So much money will secure such a lawyer, whose very name carries power with it to so influence a jury as to secure acquittal, or a disagreement, which is about equal to an acquittal. Now I would not deny the worst criminal the right to a defense; but when a crime has been committed that shocks the moral sense of even irreligious people, and when there is no doubt as to the man's guilt, then, when in answer to a call for money a lawyer lends his name, his influence, his eloquence, his wit and his wisdom in defense of that criminal, and when, by ingenuities, by unwarranted exceptions, by "packing" the jury, so as to be able to tell beforehand what the verdict will be, and by perversion of law secures the acquittal of the criminal, or has awarded him a ridiculously inadequate sentence, then I say such a lawyer—no matter what his social standing, what his qualifications—such a lawyer becomes the accomplice of criminals. He helps to undermine our social fabric, and disgraces an honorable profession.

Let the corrupt juries, the more contemptible laws, rules and practices in the impaneling of juries disappear; let the trickery of legal shysters be expelled from our courts, and the vile tribe of criminal pettifogging dudes be banished from the presence of respectable judges, and let the execution of justice be changed from a hideous sham to a reasonably swift and a reasonably certain reality, and crime will cease to walk among us with brazen face.

Undoubtedly the "blood and thunder" fiction of to-day—the books apologetic for crime—books swarming with libertines and desperadoes, are filling the minds of men with sin and whirling them into iniquity. Our newspapers daily have chronicles similar to the following: "A half dozen boys formed themselves together as a gang of road agents on the Western frontier, after the manner so graphically pictured in the popular fiction of the day." Another boy shot his step-mother. He said: "I don't see anything wrong in that kind of thing; it's dead sure to make me the hero of a novel with my picture in it." "A boy in Ohio went out into the yard and blew out his brains with a shot-gun, after a manner described in a novel he had been reading." I have the profoundest contempt for those papers which give publicity to every crime, and lionize the criminals. And the man who publishes such a paper is a cancer-planter, and beside him the lowest thief is a gentleman and the foulest tramp a prince.

Another class of books which tend to criminality are infidel books. The life of every infidel author is so polluted with shame, sensuality, debauchery and demoralizing sentiments, as to make their books, of all others, the most dangerous. Let a man read infidel books, and he will soon give up his religion, his God and his morals. Let us reject, denounce, cast out and hate with infinite scorn all infidel books.

My theme also impresses me with the fact that moral and religious education is indispensable. It is a fact that ignorance and crime abound most in those communities where the people know least of God's law; therefore, every man who seeks to destroy confidence in God's law is an enemy to his country and a promoter of crime.

Religious principle is the only moral safeguard of a man. Some years ago a country preacher, who had been appointed chaplain of the prison at Sing Sing, clumsily began his work by patting a prisoner on the back and saying: "Do you love the Lord?" The convict replied sharply: "What do you take me for? *If I had loved the Lord I shouldn't be here.*" Those who love the Lord do not dwell in prisons. I care not who or what a man may be, if he goes away from God I will not warrant that he shall not be guilty of the foulest crimes or sink to the lowest point of moral degradation. There are sad and sickening proofs around us on every side; and though every sinner does not go to the extremest length in his wanderings from God and right, yet he may do it. There is no certainty where a man will go without the restraining grace of God, and the history of every-day life proclaims it in trumpet tones, that if you neglect the principles and precepts and restraints of religion, you have no security that you will not go down—wildly down—ignominiously down—forever down. Put your trust in God, and he will put his Almighty arms under you and lift you up above the world's temptations. You will pull grandly through this life, and in death go up—gloriously up—forever up!

XX.
Dollars and Sense.

THE Bible does not say one word against making money. It tells us that money "answereth all things." It warns us against the love of money, which is "the root of all evil." It is no fancy sketch which the poet has drawn of gold and its worshipers, who

> "On its altar sacrificed ease, peace,
> Truth, faith, integrity, good conscience, friends,
> Love, charity, benevolence, and all
> The sweet and tender sympathies of life;
> And, to complete the horrid, murderous rite,
> And signalize their folly, offered up
> Their souls and an eternity of bliss,
> To gain them—what? An hour of dreaming joy,
> A feverish hour, that hastened to be done,
> And ended in the bitterness of woe."

The covetous rich man is never happy. Indescribable are his cares, griefs and fears. Theophrastus thus describes the character of a covetous man: "Lying in bed, he asked his wife whether she shut the trunks and chests fast, the cap-case be sealed, and whether the hall-door be bolted: and, though she says all is well, he riseth out of his bed in his shirt, barefooted and barelegged, to see whether it be so, with a dark lantern searching every corner, scarce sleeping a wink all night." The covetous man pines in plenty, like Tantalus up to the chin in water, yet thirsty. As the dog in Æsop's fable lost the real flesh for the shadow of it, so the covetous man casts away the true riches for the love of the shadowy. It is a common saying that a hog is good for nothing while he is alive; and so a covetous rich man does no good with his riches until he is dead and his riches come to be disposed of. Common as the folly may be, there is none greater than that of people living miserably in order to die magnificently and rich. A very rich man was told by a friend that he ought to give away his money *during his life.* He was startled by the suggestion, but said, and there was a mournful honesty in his remark : "*Oh, but you see, I would like to die rich.*" This reminds me of the poet's line :

"Hell's loudest laugh, the thought of dying rich."

Be your own executor. Do good with your money while you live. The only real way to die rich is to be rich in faith and *good works.*

When a man dies, people ask : "How much did he leave behind?" But God, who judges, will ask : "What are the good deeds which thou hast sent before thee?"

XXI.
The World Unsatisfying.

ALEXANDER THE GREAT overran the whole earth, and subdued every nation; and at the conclusion of universal victory he sat down and wept like a child because he had not another world to conquer. We read also of a Roman emperor, who had run the round of all the pleasures in the world, offering a rich reward to any one who should discover a new pleasure. Cyrus, the conqueror, thought that for a little time he was making a fine thing out of this world; yet before he came to his grave he wrote out this pitiful epitaph for his monument: "I am Cyrus. I occupied the Persian Empire. I was King over Asia. Begrudge me not this monument." But the world in after years plowed up his sepulchre. Pope Adrian VI. had this inscription on his monument: "Here lies Adrian VI., who was never so unhappy in any period of his life as at that in which he was a prince." "I, sinful wretch, by the grace of God, King of England and of France, and Lord of Ireland, bequeath to Almighty God my sinful soul and the life I have misspent, whereof I put myself wholly at his grace and mercy"—so wrote Henry IV., in his last will, when the frightful reality of leprosy had disenchanted the rapturous dream of usurpation. Queen Elizabeth, dying, cried: "Millions of money for an inch of time." Was the gay queen happy? The history of kings and queens proves that though their crowns may be "set with diamonds or Indian stones," the kings and queens themselves but seldom enjoy the crown of content which is worn upon the heart.

The world clapped its hands and stamped its feet in honor of Charles Lamb. Was he happy? He says: "I walk up and down, thinking I am happy, but feeling I am not." Samuel Johnson, happy? "No. I am afraid I shall some day get crazy." Buchanan, the world-renowned writer, exiled from his own country, appealing to Henry VIII. for protection—happy? "No. Over mountains covered with snow, and through valleys flooded with rain, I come a fugitive." "Indeed, my lord," wrote famous Edmund Burke, "I doubt whether, in these hard times, I would give a peck of refuse wheat for all that is called fame in the world." "Sweet," says the poet, "sweet were the days when I was all unknown;

> But when my name was lifted up, the storm
> Broke on the mountain, and I cared not for it."

Man's soul thirsts and longs for something nobler, brighter, greater and better than the world itself. As Macduff says: "As well try to fill the yawning chasm with a few grains of sand as satisfy the gulf of the soul's desires with the pleasures of an empty world." Nothing can satisfy the soul but God.

XXII.
Sensational Preaching.

WEBSTER thus defines "sensational:" "Attended by, or fitted to, excite great interest." If religion is the great concernment of life it ought to be presented in a way so as to excite great interest. If there is one thing that ought to make a sensation, it is the tremendous reality of eternity. Sugar-coated sermons, the prophesying of smooth things and glittering generalities never make a sensation, but facts and specifics always do. A man who goes through a sermon free from fervor or agitation; exhibits no emotion, no earnestness, no reality; makes no unguarded expressions; is faultless to a fault; makes nobody mad, and makes No. 14 shoes for No. 7 feet, will never make a sensation. I think foul scorn of conventional rhetoric and soft sentimentalism. Oh, may God make us all sensational enough to win from sin to holiness! A sensationless sermon is like gasless soda. Shakespeare says:

> "There is a divinity which shapes our ends,
> Rough hew them how we will."

So I could not do otherwise than I do if I would, and I would not if I could.

> "Ist's Gottes Werk so wird's bestehen;
> Ist's Menschen Werk wird's unter gehen."

It is said that I often say things which make people laugh. Is there anything mean in a laugh? Is there any piety in crying? Is there not sorrow enough in the world during the week, without going to church on Sunday to cry? Furthermore, are there not many churches in this city where the people sleep? Which is the greater sin, to sleep or laugh in church? The only man who ought not to smile in church is the man who has been mean during the week.

Nine-tenths of the people who came to hear Christ came from idle curiosity. The same is true of John the Baptist and nearly all of God's prophets. I admit that multitudes come here through curiosity, but under God they are given blessings of surprise, and oh, how often have we seen it true, that

"They who came to scoff, remained to pray."

Hundreds to-day, who had given up church-going for years attend here regularly with joy and devotion, and are among our best supporters and most earnest workers. But by "the help of God I continue." Hence, I thankfully and joyfully exclaim: "Not unto us, O Lord, not unto us, but unto thy name be all the glory!"

XXIII.
A Sum in Addition.

ST. PETER says: "Add to your faith virtue, and to virtue knowledge, and to knowledge temperance, and to temperance patience, and to patience godliness, and to godliness brotherly kindness, and to brotherly kindness charity."

We are not to content ourselves with a single grace. Give all diligence, make good use of every Christian advantage, and secure as high attainments as we possibly can. The graces of religion are as susceptible of cultivation as any other virtues. We are to have an accumulation of virtues and graces. It is our business to *add on* one after another, until we have become possessed of all.

Faith is mentioned first, because it is the foundation of all Christian virtues. Faith in Christ, and not a mere intellectual belief in the general existence of God, which may be said to be a universal religious sentiment. The devils believe and tremble. The belief in God is an ineradicable instinct of man's religious nature. It is incorporated in the structure and functions of his moral being. More than this, the whole universe proclaims there is a God! The herbs of the valley and the cedars of the mountain bless him; each bird and insect that lives and moves proclaims him. The seas roar him, the winds whisper him, the storm thunders him, and the ocean proclaims his immensity. Man's own moral nature responds to this truth; reason demands and accepts it; conscience announces and enforces it. The fool alone has said in his heart, not his head, there is no God. A belief in God's existence is inevitable, and there is nothing praiseworthy or meritorious for a man to believe on God.

Neither is there anything praiseworthy in a general belief in the historical existence of Jesus Christ, as recorded in the Gospels. An intellectual acceptance of the mere facts of Christ's life and death is not saving or Gospel faith. Every man, who believes in history at all, is obliged to believe in the existence of Christ, whether he wishes to or not. There is no escaping it, except by a universal historical skepticism.

Saving faith is unreservedly surrendering to Christ as our *personal Lord and Redeemer;* taking him as our master and model; obeying his words as the law and guide of our life.

"Add to your faith *virtue.*" Virtue here has reference to the common meaning of the Greek word, as referring to manliness, firmness and independence. Many men's gentleness is the gentleness of weakness. The Christian must have strength of conviction and force of character. Gentleness can be overdone. We have need to add to the patience of Job the meekness of Moses, the amiability of John, the sharp words and shaggy mien of Elijah and John the Baptist, the boldness of Peter, the enthusiasm of Paul, the bluntness of Latimer, the severity of Knox, and the magnificent explosions of Luther's far-resounding indignation.

Some blurt forth their feelings rudely, and apologize for their roughness by calling it honesty, straightforwardness and plainness of speech. Now, we can be explicit and open, and honest, and withal courteous and considerate of the feelings of others. We can add to fidelity brotherly kindness. No one was ever more plain in speech, more faithful and certain in reproof, than Christ; but his love infused every warning. We can be strong characters, men of remarkable decision, inflexible purpose, aye, even be stirred with the anger that is as majestic as the frown of Jehovah's brow—the anger of truth and love—without renouncing the meekness and gentleness which were in Christ.

"And to virtue *knowledge.*" The knowledge of God and salvation through the Redeemer. It is the duty of every Christian to make the highest possible attainments in *knowledge.* We should know as much of Christ as it is possible for us to know. The greatest object of Paul's desire was to know Christ, to become as fully acquainted as he could with his character, his plans, with the relations which he sustained to the Father, and with the claims of his religion. To *know* Christ is the greatest privilege of the Christian.

In the Royal Gallery at Dresden there is a painting of the Divine Child, by Raphael, that is more admired for its beauty than any other like production. There was a tourist who was so charmed by this picture that, day by day, for two months, he stood before the wonderful conception, spell-bound, occasionally weeping with delight as some new beauty would appear, and when his last day had arrived, and his horses were ready for the road, he ran back and took a parting gaze. We have the original of that picture in the four Gospels, sketched from life. Here behold Him, not on canvas, but the living, loving, acting Jesus. Study this portrait. Strive to know more of Christ. Nothing will prompt you so much to a life of self-denial; nothing will make you so benevolent and so alive to the highest and best interests of the world.

"And to knowledge *temperance*." The word temperance here refers to the mastery over all our evil inclinations and appetites. "Temperate in all things"—in sleep, in food, in drink, in speech, in business, in pastime, in everything. We are to confine everything within proper limits, and to no propensity of our nature are we to give indulgence beyond the limits which the law of God allows.

The temperance cause should not be based upon a philological argument over a disputed word, nor on the debatable ground that drinking pure wine is a sin in itself. The wine that Christ made and drank was not the fiery and poisonous compound of modern distillation and manufacture. The wine of Palestine was light, pure wine. It was the usual beverage of that land; and that drunkenness was rare is evident from the fact that there is no rebuke of it anywhere in the Gospels, or any reference to its existence. And not until we come to the Epistles of Paul, and to the customs and habits of the Gentiles, do we find temperance exhortations; and he gives this reason for abstinence: Charity to the weak. He says: "*All things are lawful, but all things are not expedient. It is good neither to eat flesh nor to drink wine, nor anything whereby thy brother is offended or made weak.*"

"And to temperance *patience*." I do not take patience in this connection to mean simply enduring trial without murmuring, complaining or rebelling, in order that the effects of affliction should produce in the soul the results which trials are adapted to accomplish. We are to exercise our opportunities for the play of good nature. We are not to be irritable, huffy, sensitive. We should not lose our temper. We live only by the forbearance of God. We are to repeat in our lives, as his children at least, something of this patience. We are taught to pray every day : " Forgive us our debts, *as we forgive* our debtors." If we are exacting and revengeful, if we cannot forgive the unkind treatment of others, how can we sincerely pray this petition ?

" And to patience *godliness.*" True piety : reverencing God, his character and his laws; obeying him from love. Godliness is forming and influencing our life by a regard for God.

" And to godliness *brotherly kindness.*" Kindness is the sun of life. Give no pain. Say not a word, give not the expression of the countenance that will offend another, or send a thrill of pain to his bosom. Kindness is the charm with which the Christian should captivate, and the sword with which to conquer. How true it is that

> " A little word in kindness spoken,
> A motion or a tear,
> Has often healed the heart that's broken,
> And made a friend sincere !"

Cherish a bright, sunny, cheerful temper and disposition.

" And to brotherly kindness *charity.*" Charity is the brightest star in the Christian's diadem. With Cotton, let us pray:

> " Fair charity be thou my guest,
> And be thy constant couch my breast."

Charity "thinketh no evil." With an unwilling ear and sad heart it hears bad news. It glories in no man's misfortune. It rather holds down its head and partakes of his shame. It rejoices in the belief that everybody is sincere. Where it cannot succor want, it will condole.

> " Soft peace it brings wherever it arrives;
> It builds our quiet, latent hope revives,
> Lays the rough paths of nature smooth and even,
> And opens in each breast a little heaven."

XXIV.
Sleeping Under the Sermon.

IN *Acts* xx : 9, we read: *"And there sat in a window a certain young man, named Eutychus, being fallen into a deep sleep; and as Paul was long preaching, he sunk down with sleep, and fell down from the third loft, and was taken up dead."*

For what purpose is this paragraph here? That preachers should not preach long sermons? Paul did not consider it such a warning, for, as soon as the young man was restored, he began again and preached until the gray streaks of dawn lit up the Eastern sky. If, however, a tedious preacher should quote Paul's example, it may be sufficient to remind him that he is not a great apostle.

Paul was such an interesting preacher that the hours flew unobserved. He was born in the famous university town of Tarsus; versed in the Stoic philosophy, as his sermons amply show; learned besides in all the wisdom of the Jewish schools; he associated with men like Apollos, skilled rhetoricians; he sought the aid of all the culture of the day, and thus his audience was carried away by his solid thought, irresistible logic, attractive style, bold novelty, burning eloquence, and overpowering earnestness.

We learn further from this narrative *the importance of social worship.* They were not satisfied with being Christians on their own account; reading and praying in private did not satisfy them. And the man who is satisfied to stay away from the church surely has his heart in the wrong place, and will soon be numbered among the backsliders. The apostle warns us "not to forsake the assembling of ourselves together."

We learn also that *the first day of the week was set apart for religious worship*. "On the first day of the week, when the disciples came together." In honor of Christ's resurrection, the Sabbath was changed from the seventh to the first day of the week. Christ, during his forty days on earth after his resurrection, appeared to his disciples in every instance on the first day of the week. On the first day of the week Christ founded his church. Among the apostles it was the chosen day for worship. John began turning the prophetic wheel on "the Lord's Day," a term applied by the Church Fathers to designate the day on which the Lord arose. Listen to the historic evidence of the founders, defenders and leaders of the church of the first centuries. Justin Martyr says: "*On Sunday* do the saints assemble." Ignatius says: "Let us no more Sabbatize, but keep the Lord's Day." Irenæus says: "*On the Lord's Day* every one of us Christians keeps the Sabbath." Clement, of Alexandria, declares that: "The keeping of the Lord's Day is incumbent on Christians." And Origen says: "*The Lord's Day* ought to be preferred to the Jewish Sabbath." The Christian Sabbath was founded by Christ, established by the apostles, and indorsed by the voice of history. Let us ever keep it holy unto the Lord.

The duty and privilege of the Lord's supper is also taught here. In primitive times all who took upon themselves the Christian name sat down together at the holy feast. All who assembled in the upper room at Troas met to join in the ordinance, Eutychus amongst the rest. O! ye who bear the Christian name, never absent yourselves from the Lord's table. Nothing will strengthen you so much for the battle of life.

I also gather from this passage that *preaching is an important part of divine worship*. A great many of our churches are nothing but horticultural exhibitions and appendixes to a concert. The liturgy is accounted all; and a ten minutes' essay, whose only redeeming feature often is its brevity, takes the place of instructive exposition of God's word, or impassioned appeal. We shall do well to stick to apostolic times, and enforce the great doctrines of Christian faith and morals.

XXV.
Calvin and Calvinism.

PRESBYTERIANS are not called "Calvinists" because they are followers of Calvin in doctrine or in discipline. We "build upon the foundation of the apostles and prophets, Jesus Christ himself being the chief corner-stone." We are Christians in doctrine, Presbyterians in polity—the only polity known to the apostles and primitive Christians. The doctrines of Calvin were not originated by him. They existed and were adopted previous to Calvin; but he so well defended, so clearly expounded, and so perfectly systematized these principles as to connect with them his illustrious name. Renan sarcastically said: "Paul begat Augustine, and Augustine begat Calvin." But who begat Paul? Our theology was born in heaven. Its paternity is from God.

Though we call no man "our father," yet we are proud of John Calvin. The Lutheran Reformation traveled but little out of Germany and the Scandinavian kingdoms, while Calvinism obtained a European character. Under Calvin Geneva became the capital of European reform and the cradle of civil and religious liberty. Calvin was a politician as well as a theologian. He made the ecclesiastical tribunals independent of the civil law, and through his teachings Geneva became the fertile seed-plot of popular liberty and republicanism.

The Calvinistic preachers kindled the fire of liberty into a blaze, and made tyranny and despotism lick the dust. Calvinism intoxicated Europe with republicanism. The convulsion in France, the confederation of the States of Holland, the revolutionizing of England and Scotland were due to Calvinism.

Calvinists founded this great, growing and glorious Republic. The Pilgrims of Plymouth Rock, the Puritans of Massachusetts, the Holland Reformers of New York, and the Scotch-Irish Presbyterians of North Carolina, who were the first to declare for independence, were Calvinists. Had it not been for these Calvinists—these Christian patriots—American independence would have found its grave, rather than a recognition before the world. George Bancroft, author of "The History of the United States," says: "He that will not honor the memory and respect the influence of Calvin, knows but little of the origin of American liberty."

"Again, we boast of our common school system. Calvin was the father of popular education, and the inventor of the system of free schools."

Ranke says: "John Calvin was virtually the founder of America." Froude, the great English historian, says: "John Calvin has done more for constitutional liberty than any other man." And when I remember that the Church of England attempted to found a State Church in Virginia to the exclusion of every other, I thank God for the Calvinists who fought that this might be a country where every man could worship God according to the dictates of his conscience. As a lover of American liberty, I thank God for John Calvin and Calvinism, for to their influence I owe the liberty wherein I now stand and rejoice.

XXVI.
The Bible and History.

THE Bible accords in a most wonderful manner with ancient history. There is nothing more common in history than the recognition of a God. The fictions of the poets respecting the different ages of the world coincide with the facts of Scripture. The first, or Golden Age, is a feeble representation of the bliss of our first parents (*Gen.* ii.), and the second, or Iron Age, described in the fiction of Pandora and her fatal box of evils, which overspread the earth, is in accordance with the introduction of evil into the world (*Gen.* iii.). Similar accounts of the creation are found among the ancient Phœnicians, and among the ancient Greek philosophers.

In all the superstitions of the world you find evidences of man's fall, of a serpent being the instrument in it, of propitiatory sacrifices, and longing for a deliverer. That the aspect of the globe has been entirely changed is an undisputed fact. The oldest nation on earth—the Chinese—have a tradition almost exactly similar to that of Moses, in these words: "The pillars of heaven were broken; the earth shook to its foundations; the heavens sunk lower towards the North; the sun, the moon and the stars changed their motions; the earth fell to pieces, and the waters inclosed within its bosom burst forth with violence and overflowed it. Man having rebelled against heaven, the system of the universe was totally disordered.

and the grand harmony of nature was disturbed." The long lives of men in the early age of the world are mentioned by Berosus, Manetho, Hesiodus and others.

And with respect to the New Testament, we have the testimony of Josephus, Tacitus and Suetonius, that Christ existed and was crucified at the time in which the evangelists place that event. Celsus, born A. D. 150, full of enmity to the Christian religion, mentions so many circumstances in Christ's history, that his life might almost be taken from the very fragments of Celsus's book, preserved by Origen, which never pretends to dispute Christ's real existence, or the facts recorded of him.

THE PRESERVATION OF THE BIBLE.

That the Jews neither mutilated nor corrupted the Scriptures is fully proven by the silence of the prophets, as well as of Christ and his apostles, who, though they bring many charges against them, never once accuse them of corrupting one of their sacred writings; and also by the agreement in every essential point of all the versions and manuscripts, amounting to nearly 1150, which are now extant, and which furnish a clear proof of their uncorrupted preservation. As to the New Testament, Lord Hailes, of Scotland, searched the writings of the Church Fathers to the end of the third century, and he actually found *the whole of the New Testament* (with the exception of less than a dozen verses) scattered through their writings, which are still extant; so that, had every copy of the New Testament been annihilated at the Council of Nice, A. D. 325, when infidels say the New Testament was compiled, the book could have been reproduced from the writings of the early Church Fathers, who quoted the book then as we quote it now, and *believed it then as we believe it now.*

Moses wrote 1500 B. C. Confucius lived 600 B. C.—nine hundred years after Moses. On the authority of Max Müller, the Vedas are not older than 1200 before Christ. The oldest human compilation, that of Zoroaster, is 300 years younger than the five books of Moses, and the outgrowth of them.

Who can account for the Mosaic septenary division of time having its imagery in the history, mythology and philosophy of the race ? No natural change points out such a measure as is the case with the month and year, and yet it has been employed as a sacred number by people most diversified in habit, and most remote from each other in time and place.

The proof of the antiquity of the Mosaic record is also found in the language of every country in the world. Words such as Adam and Eve all indicate the Hebrew to have been the language of Eden. Every one acquainted with the Hebrew tongue, the Greek and Latin, and modern languages, will see that most of them can more or less plainly be traced back to the Hebrew. The very letters of the Hebrew alphabet—*aleph, beth, gimel, daleth,* etc.—are exactly parallel with the Greek *alpha, beta, gamma, delta,* etc., and if we refer to the English alphabet, or the Italian, French, Spanish and German, we find nearly the same form given to the letters, and almost the same sounds, and all corresponding strikingly with the Hebrew. This proves that languages look back to the first—the Hebrew; that the language of every nation owns the Hebrew as its parent. In short, the languages of the world reflect the unquestionably historical antiquity, the divine inspiration and truth of the Mosaic record.

THE BIBLE AND LIBERTY.

The oldest and best pyramid that can be erected to liberty is Christianity. Wherever Bible readers and Bible believers are in the ascendency, or numerically in the majority, there will be found the greatest amount of both physical and intellectual liberty, and the greatest freedom of thought, speech and action. The countries that are indisputably the foremost and most enlightened of all other nations are Bible countries. On the other hand, where skepticism prevails, and especially in the communities where it is in the ascendency, there will be found nihilism, communism, and the greatest amount of despotism. Why is it that the most highly civilized and intelligent people, the most just and reasonable laws, and the broadest liberty are to be found only in Bible countries? And why is it that in those countries where the Bible has not yet come the people are generally ignorant, their laws crude and oppressive, and their rulers despots? Is it not a fact that liberty finds her only place of abode in Bible countries? And if intelligence, liberty, and civilization exist only in the highest sense where an open Bible is found, what guarantee have we that, if the Bible should be destroyed, the things which we now love more than anything else in the world will not vanish with it? The friends of liberty first met in the sacred temple of God, and liberty, conceived by the Bible, was born upon the holy altar of the Christian church. She worships at her august shrine, and bows with imperial grandeur before her majestic throne.

XXVII.
Pride.

PRIDE is a virtue. Pride is also a vice. Without pride as a principle a man cannot be virtuous. The pride that is a vice is the overvaluing of one's self for some real or imagined superiority, producing haughty bearing and arrogance of manner.

It is related of the French family of the Duke de Levis, that they have a picture of their pedigree, in which Noah is represented going into the ark, and carrying a small trunk, on which is written: "Papers belonging to the Levis family." There are many men whose reputation hangs upon their having had a grandfather, and the only thing they do is talk about their noble ancestry.

The peacock has graceful hues, that put to shame the richest fabrics ever wrought in looms. Could he but look at his ugly feet his pride would soon abate. So with men: if there be beauty, rank, wealth, fame, talent, success, or any other thing that will engender pride, there is also some counterpart to it to keep them humble. Some shrewd philosopher has said that if the best man had his faults written on his forehead they would make him pull his hat over his eyes!

Wordsworth asks:

> "What is pride? A whizzing rocket
> That would emulate a star."

There is a plenty of ragged aristocracy in the world—gaudy parlors and empty kitchens. Trying to be somebody when you are nobody is up-hill work.

Solomon says: "Pride goeth before destruction, and a haughty spirit before a fall." When once a philosopher was asked what the great God was doing, he replied: "His whole employment is to lift up the humble and to cast down the proud."

One of Æsop's fables says that there was a tortoise once that was very unhappy, because he had no wings and could not fly. As he saw the eagles and other birds having a good time floating through the air, he said to himself: "O, if I only had wings as those birds have, so that I could rise up into the air and sail about there as they do, how happy I should be!" One day, the fable says, he called to an eagle and offered him a great reward if he would only teach him how to fly. "I never shall be happy," said the tortoise, "till I get wings and fly about in the air as you do." The eagle told him he had no wings to give him and did not know how to teach him to fly. But the tortoise pressed him so earnestly, and made him so many promises, that finally the eagle said: "Well, I'll try what I can do. You get on my back and I'll carry you up in the air, and we'll see what can be done."

So the tortoise got on the back of the eagle. Then the eagle spread out his wings and began to soar aloft. He went up, and up, and up, till he had reached a great height. Then he said to the tortoise: "Now get ready; I'm going to throw you off, and you must try your hand at flying." So the eagle threw him off, and he went down, and down, and down, till at last he fell upon a hard rock and was dashed to pieces. Proud ambition to fly has cost many people their lives. "Be content with such things as ye have."

Pride is the offspring of want of merit. Humility is the child of wisdom. Solomon says: "Before honor is humility;" and Christ says: "He that humbleth himself shall be exalted."

The stalks of wheat that hold up their heads so high are empty-headed, and those which hang down their heads modestly are full of precious grain. The people who hold their heads so high do so because they have not sense enough to weigh them down.

Feltham says: "Of all the trees, I observe that God hath chosen the vine—a low plant that creeps upon the helpful wall; of all the beasts, the soft and pliant lamb; of all the fowls, the mild and guileless dove. When God appeared to Moses it was not in the lofty cedar, nor in the spreading palm, but a bush—a humble, abject bush."

> "The bird that soars on highest wing,
>   Builds on the ground her lowly nest;
> And she that doth most sweetly sing,
>   Sings in the shade when all things rest:
> In lark and nightingale we see
> What honor hath humility.
>
> "The saint that wears heaven's brightest crown,
>   In deepest adoration bends;
> The weight of glory bows him down
>   The most when most his soul ascends:
> Nearest the throne itself must be
> The footstool of humility."

XXVIII.
Honoring Our Parents.

THE religion of the Chinese consists in honoring their ancestors. One good result flows from their religion: they do not speak disrespectfully of their parents. They do not call their father "the old man," or "the governor." They do not call their mother "the old woman." May not this be the reason why God has given China so long a life as a nation?

Obey your parents: not from fear, but from love. Too many children obey because they know what will come if they don't. They obey because they must or get punished. Mothers are often fretful and fathers tyrants and despots, from whom there is no appeal, provoking their children to wrath, which God forbids.

Obey your parents because you love them, because it is right, and because God asks it. Let your obedience be prompt and cheerful.

Obey your parents in their absence. So act in their absence that you can always in their presence look them right in the eye.

Treat your parents' wish as though it were a command. When George Washington was all ready to go to sea, he discovered that his mother did not wish him to go. As he went in to say good-bye to her, he found her in tears. That was enough for him. He went out and said to his servant: "Take my trunk back again to my room; I will not break my mother's heart to please myself."

When his mother heard what he had done she said: "George, God has promised to bless those who honor their parents, and he will bless you!" And God *did* bless Washington, and made him a blessing to the world. When he conquered himself he won a greater victory than when he conquered the British at Trenton and at Monmouth and at Yorktown. Washington's obedience to his parents was the turning-point in his life and led to all his after-greatness.

The Hon. Thomas H. Benton was for thirty years a United States Senator. When making a speech in New York once, he turned to the ladies present, and spoke thus about his mother: "My mother asked me never to use tobacco, and I have never touched it from that day to this. She asked me never to learn to gamble, and I never learned to gamble. When I was seven years old, she asked me not to drink, and I made a resolution of total abstinence. That resolution I have never broken. And now whatever service I may have been able to render to my country, or whatever honor I may have gained, I owe it to my mother." Find out what the wishes of your parents are and follow them.

Obey your parents in the Lord. God is above your parents. They have no right to command you to do what God forbids.

Help your parents all you can. Remember what they have done for you. When you were helpless they helped you; now when they are helpless help them. Save them as many steps as you can. A young lady will never miss it in marrying a young man who is kind and devoted to his mother. The young lady who sits at the piano and sings "What is Home Without a Mother?" when the mother in question is doing all the hard work, will never make a good wife.

Remember this, too, that a son's or daughter's spotless name is, while life lasts, a father's truest glory and a mother's greatest joy.

Help your parents in old age. Make them comfortable. The young man or the young woman who is ashamed of his or her father or mother because the brilliance has faded out of the eyes and the roses have fled from the cheeks, is a grown-up baby. Visit your parents as often as you can. Cheer them in their declining days. If you cannot visit them, write to them often. Amid all the successes of the noble Garfield, nothing stirred his energy more than the thought of the gratification that would be given to his mother's heart. He always found time to write a letter home and tell all that he was doing.

Christ, while suffering on the cross, provided a home and a guardian for his mother: "Now, when Jesus therefore saw his mother and the disciple standing by, whom he loved, he saith unto his mother: Behold thy son! And from that hour the disciple took her into his own home." How beautifully this sets the example of Christ before us to teach us how to honor our father and mother!

XXIX.
Hypocritical Punctiliousness.

THERE are people so very punctilious in the observance of all acts of worship and devotion who, in their practical life, are little better than the heathen. Conscientiousness in little things in regard to ecclesiastical etiquette will not cover personal sins. There are people so decorous in their behavior in the house of God, that to smile would be to sin; whose hearts are full of envy, jealousy and bitterness. If you have been a good citizen, a kind neighbor, a true friend, a dutiful son, a faithful husband, and walked humbly with God during the week, go to the house of God on Sunday with a bright and merry face.

There are people so sanctimonious that they would not blacken their boots on Sunday, but will blacken their reputations during the week. They won't shave on Sunday, but shave their neighbors to the tune of twenty per cent. during the week. They would not ride on the street-cars on Sunday, but will ride the men in their employ to death during the week. "Consistency, thou art a jewel," and a jewel few people can wear.

There are many overearnest men who have no doubt but that the whole universe of truth is inclosed within the sweep of their own little pair of compasses, and who feel that they are placed at heaven's gate—namely, their church—to protect it from the entrance of unworthy applicants. The punctiliousness of our churches is not only a stumbling-block to the timid, but to all who hold themselves superior in things of the soul to human dictation, and especially the inquisitorial and offensive dictation of bigots.

Religion is not church-going; it is not going to a particular church; it is not singing out of a particular hymn-book; it is not being orthodox and going among men as orthodox, and sending the people to perdition who do not believe as you do. Instead of making more noise in the world about our orthodoxy than the Master ever did, and elaborate and ostentatious prayers, as to be troublesome to our neighbor, let us fear God and do righteousness from Sunday to Sunday, and from Monday to Monday. He is the true believer who is the subject of high and divine inspirations, so deep and profound that he cannot utter them, and not he who is loaded and clogged with the mere theories of dead men on the subject, that leave no scope for anything else.

> * " 'Tis not the wise phylactery,
> Nor stubborn taste, nor stated prayers,
> That makes us saints; we judge the tree
> By what it bears."

XXX.
The Lawyers.

THERE are many dishonorable lawyers, just as there are many dishonorable men in all professions and callings. I cannot, in the light of history and justice, join in the popular derisive cry against lawyers. The law as a profession is an honorable profession, and contains many of the world's most honored and honorable names. As a lover of freedom, I gratefully remember what lawyers have done for humanity. Turn the pages of history and go back with me to Greece. A lawyer, Demosthenes, the world's greatest orator, was the greatest champion of freedom and the rights of the people. It was Cicero, a lawyer, who exposed the conspiracy of Catiline, and stood up for the rights of the people. Henry Grattan and Daniel O'Connell, lawyers, gave to down-trodden, bleeding, suffering Ireland what little liberty she has to-day. It was Lord Brougham, a lawyer, who gave to England popular education. It was Patrick Henry, a young lawyer, who stood upon the floor of the Virginia House of Burgesses (second only to the Scotch-Irish Presbyterians of North Carolina), to fire the hearts of our forefathers to strike for independence, and amidst cries of "treason" uttered these words: "Tarquin and Cæsar had each his Brutus, Charles I. his Cromwell, and George III. may profit by their example." It was John Adams, a lawyer, who stood up so bravely in the Continental Congress for the rights of the people.

Thomas Jefferson, the man who wrote the grandest document ever penned, was a lawyer. When South Carolina threatened to trail our flag in the dirt, the man who spoke in eloquent strains that still thrill the hearts of the American people to enthusiastic loyalty was Daniel Webster, a lawyer. That grand man, the emancipator of four million slaves, the martyr to freedom, Abraham Lincoln, was a lawyer. And up on the rock-pillared Sinai, and among the shaded hills of Galilee, we behold the fountains whence all law sprung—Moses and Christ.

XXXI.
Force of Character.

A VIRTUOUS woman is an evangel of goodness to the world. She is one of the pillars in the eternal kingdom of right. The world would go to ruin without the influence of woman's moral and religious character. But woman does not do enough. Her power is not equal to its need. The world is a grand Pandora's box of wickedness—a far-spread scene of selfishness and sensualism, in which woman herself acts a conspicuous part. There is to-day a loud call for a more active religion—a more powerful impulse in behalf of morality. To youthful women we must look for a leader in the cause of morality and religion. The girls of to-day are greatly instrumental in giving a beautiful complexion to the society of to-morrow.

Why do not the women of to-day exercise that same moral sway over their male associates that our fathers tell us our mothers did over them? Because they do not possess sufficient force of character. Their moral wills are not resolute. Their influence is not armed with executive power. They would not have a drunkard for a husband, but they will drink a glass of wine with a young man in our fashionable restaurants or hotels, on the way home from the theatre. They would not take the name of God in vain, but they love the society of men who swear like troopers out of their presence. They would not be dishonest, but they exaggerate and equivocate, and affect and pretend, so that many men seldom think of believing what young women tell them. They countenance the society of tricksters and deceivers, and allow a ten-dollar-a-week society swell to spend twice that amount on them for theatre tickets, carriages, flowers, etc., when they know, or ought to know, that these things are unpaid for, employers robbed, or appearances kept up by borrowing or sponging. They would not be irreligious, but they smile upon men who boast that for years they had not been inside of a church, and sneer at God and divine things, and proclaim themselves "free thinkers." They would not be licentious, but have no stunning rebuke for men whose very touch is pollution, and admit them into their society.

This is the virtue of too many women. We need women who will regard their moral convictions as solemn resolves to be true to God and duty, come what may. A young lady by her constant and consistent Christian example can exert an untold power for good, and in this way only can she make the young man believe that her religion is the thing for him. Associate with men of intelligence and sense; with men whose language is chaste and good, whose sentiments are lofty and edifying, and whose deportment is such as correct morals dictate. She is truly beautiful who can gather the good around her for the blessing of her smiles, and strew men's pathways with moral light. Fair to God is she who teaches the sentiments of duty and honesty in every act of her life.

XXXII.
Funeral Reform.

IT is high time that we had reform in our funeral customs. I never heard of a funeral sermon converting a sinner, silencing a scoffer, or turning an infidel to the truth. Funeral sermons are often far from the truth. Generally, the less good a man has done, the more good the preacher is expected to say of him. I give you fair warning that I will not lie at your funeral; and if you insist on a sermon, I will tell the truth about you. The most sacred place to hold a funeral service is quietly in the home. There let the pastor briefly administer the comforts of religion to those who mourn.

Common decency should lead us to do away with displays which make funerals so expensive that to die costs more than to live.

Let the last parting be too sacred to be done before the eyes of an often critical and unsympathetic crowd who come from curiosity. Brass bands at a funeral are unpardonable nuisances. Loud demonstrations should be avoided.

"Stillest waters are deepest."

To hold the funerals of haters of the church in the church is wrong. It is trying to do for their bodies what they never would do for their souls. Furthermore, it seems like an injustice to the dead man. It seems like taking a mean advantage of a man after he is dead to take him by force where he could not be persuaded to go while he was alive. If a man live and die like a brute, like Jehoiakim, he should be " buried with the burial of an ass: drawn and cast forth beyond the gates of Jerusalem." Sunday funerals are rarely necessary. They nearly always assume a magnitude that amounts to Sabbath desecration. The Lord's Day is for rest and divine worship, and not for great funeral pageants.

XXXIII.
Evolution.

TWENTY-TWO hundred years ago, when the world had almost wholly apostatized from the true and living God, Democritus, among the Greeks, became offended with the gods, and set himself to invent a plan of the world without them. From Eastern travelers the Greeks knew that the Brahmans in India had a theory of the world developing itself from a primeval egg. He set himself to refine upon it, and imagined virtually the nebular hypothesis. He said that matter was eternal, and consisted of very small atoms, dancing about in all directions, and which at last happened into the various forms of the present world.

The ancient Phœnicians held a theory that all life sprung from the mud watered by the sea. Lucretius developed this theory in a poem in six books. Evolution is an old heathen mummy, and modern infidels will have their hands full galvanizing it.

The evolutionist says that infinite ages ago there existed a few primal germs (who made the primal germs these men do not know), and these primal germs developed all the living creatures of the ages. First, there was a vegetable stuff; that vegetable stuff developed into something like a jelly-fish; the jelly-fish developed into a tadpole; the tadpole developed into a snail; the snail developed into a turtle; the turtle developed into a wolf; the wolf developed into a dog; the dog developed into a monkey, and the monkey developed into a man. As Hugh Miller makes a plain farmer say on this evolution of man from the monkey : "It takes a *great deal of believing to believe that!*" But then the man who wants to get rid of God is willing to persuade himself to believe any miracle, only so it is not in the Bible.

The evolutionist counts by fossils and upheavals, and tells us that this world is millions of years old. Now, in all the millions of years covered by human history, an instance has never been known where a monkey of the highest type has given an existence to one of these self-styled infidel philosophers. No menagerie or zoological garden can be found where anything approaching the development of an infidel has occurred in the cages of monkeydom. Nor do travelers in any part of the globe bring back tidings of any portion of the world where monkeys have gone into the business of raising agnostics—*knownothings*—to deny the existence of God and sneer at Christianity.

A few days ago I met an evolutionist. I put a question to him; a question which is (d)evolution in a nutshell. I asked him : Was your mother a monkey ? He turned on his heels and left as rapidly as he could carry himself. I claim a nobler origin. With the psalmist I say : "For Thou hast made man a little lower than the angels, and hast crowned him with glory and honor."

XXXIV.
Hell in the Light of Common Sense.

THE doctrine of hell is perhaps the hardest to be received of all the articles of the Christian creed. There is reason for this. All men feel themselves guilty, and their consciences tell them that if there be such a place, unless they fall out with the devil and fall in with the angels, they will be candidates for admission, whose claims will never be disputed.

* * *

The wisest and best men of every nation and every age, the most celebrated heathen sages, who had nothing but the light of nature to guide them, as well as Jews and Christians, have stood in awe of retribution after death. And this fact of itself ought to shake the unbelief of the most intelligent skeptic. He may be very wise, but he will surely admit that men far wiser than he have arrived at conclusions exactly the opposite of those at which he arrived. Think for yourself by all means. But we believe with Lucretius, the Roman poet and philosopher, that while "it is a pleasure to stand upon the shore and to see ships tossed upon the sea, a pleasure to stand in the window of a castle and to see a battle and the adventure thereof below, yet no pleasure is comparable to the standing upon the vantage-ground of truth, and to see the errors, and the wanderings, and the mists, and the tempests in the vale below." Remember that, while in the multitudes of counselors there is safety, the man who always confides in his own judgment invariably brings himself to grief. A sound and sensible private judgment will in many things of importance and difficulty be distrustful of itself, and feel that there are other judgments at least as worthy of confidence; and, therefore, I submit the question: If nearly all the truly wise and good men of every nation and age, with all their differences of opinion upon other points, have unanimously agreed as to a future state of retribution, does not this fact claim every man's respectful attention? Can a man who wishes to have credit for good common sense say that the belief in hell is nothing more than a superstition, or an invention of preachers to make an easy living?

* * *

The question, Is there a hell? resolves itself into this: Is there a Moral Governor of the world? Is there a moral law? Is there such a thing as sin? For, if there be, then there is such a thing as punishment for sin. There is sin, and there is punishment for sin, which we daily witness. But there is not for all sin such a reckoning in this world as meets the claims of righteousness and justice. Do we not daily see evil doings pass undetected, and many bad men pass unpunished? See how often the righteous suffer and the wicked flourish. The wicked are not plagued as other men; they have more than heart can wish for. When we take a deliberate view we are naturally led to exclaim: " Wherefore do the wicked live, become old, yea, are mighty in power? Is there no reward for the righteous? Is there no punishment for the workers of iniquity? Is there no God that judgeth in the earth?" And, indeed, were there no retribution beyond the limits of this present life, we should be necessarily obliged to admit one or the other of the following

HELL IN THE LIGHT OF COMMON SENSE. 113

conclusions: either that no Moral Governor of the world exists, or that justice and judgment are not the habitation of His throne.

* * *

It is absurd to say that men are punished by the stings of conscience. If conscience have not power enough to deter men from wrong-doing, it will not have power to punish them when the wrong is done. Many a man has prospered in his wickedness, gone to his grave in peace, and experienced, even in the prospect of death, no avenging terrors, no retributive remorse. What does our sense of justice say? That such men ought to be punished, and that if they go unpunished it is wrong, and that if there be no hell there ought to be.

* * *

A heaven without a hell is an impossibility. The existence of a pure city necessarily implies the existence of impure commons, where everything impure and unfit to be in the city is cast.

* * *

Give to the justice of heaven the same common sense that you give to the justice of earth, and you will have a penitentiary somewhere in the next world.

* * *

Deny future retribution, and it is not in your power to forfeit heaven or stay out of it, live as you please; and you must expect to have as your immortal associates all the base villains that ever disgraced humanity. Is not this revolting to every feeling of propriety? Does it not contradict conscience, stultify reason, and trample every instinct of man under foot?

* * *

Where is hell? Anywhere outside of heaven. If hell be only a state, it will be hell all the same. That " there is no peace to the wicked," is a fact founded in the very constitution of man. *Sin destroys happiness.* The sinner is his own destroyer. He punishes himself. Death makes no change in our moral character. It disengages the soul from the trammels of the body and gives expansion to its powers; but he that was "unjust will be unjust still," though removed from earth to the world of spirits. The passions and propensities of the soul follow it into eternity, so that even if there were no condemnation from God, still the sinner would be in hell. In this world a man's happiness depends upon the state of his mind, and the passions of the soul will accompany it into the next world and form a part of its very being. They will there have the same influence upon our happiness as here. In order that the blind man may enjoy the beauties of the flower-garden his eyes must be opened; in order that the deaf man may enjoy the sweet strains of music his ears must be unstopped; in order that the dyspeptic may enjoy a good meal his health must be restored; and so, in order that a man may enjoy the blessings of heaven he must have his heart changed and be brought into sympathy with God, or else he would feel in heaven like a fish out of water. If there were no day of judgment and no hell, the sinner, continuing the enemy of God, must be lost and wretched. Man carries in his bosom the elements of woe, and the circumstances in which he will be placed will call them into action.

* * *

The Scripture hell-fire of torment is not material, but symbolical of mental affliction, which consists in the loss of God, of friends, of hope. Dante's poetry, his imagery of brimstone and fire must not be confused with orthodoxy. Let the memory alone of the impenitent survive, and the words of Milton will be true:

"Which way I climb is hell; myself am hell."

Memory will be the unquenchable fire, and the worm that never dies.

* * *

When we speak of hell, we call it all hell, indifferently and without distinction. There are great differences of constitution and of temperament, and there must be necessarily corresponding differences of moral obligation. That which is a temptation to one produces in another the feeling of intense disgust. Our natural capacities, our means of obtaining knowledge, our various aids to assist us in the pursuit of it, the different natures and qualities of our actions, will all be taken into consideration, and we will be rewarded or punished according to the deeds done in the body.

* * *

Christ will not let the devil have more in hell than there will be in heaven. For then Satan would laugh at Christ. In the Father's house are many mansions. St. John tells us that there will be a host beyond all count who will get into heaven. Why should not *you* then be saved? We quote the following to cheer up the disconsolate: "And he measured the city with a reed, twelve thousand furlongs. The length, height and breadth of it are equal." —*Rev.* xxi: 16. "Twelve thousand furlongs—7,920,000 feet—which, being cubed, is 948,988,000,000,000,000,-000,000 cubic feet, the half of which we will reserve for the throne of God and the court of heaven, half of the balance for the streets, and the remainder, divided by 4.96, the cubical feet in the rooms (nineteen feet square and sixteen feet high), will be 5,743,758,000,000 rooms. We will now suppose the world always did and always will contain 900,000,000 inhabitants, and a generation will last $33\frac{1}{3}$ years (2,700,000 every century), and that the world will stand a hundred thousand years—27,000,-000,000,000 persons. Then suppose there were 11,230 such worlds, equal to this number of inhabitants and duration of years: then there would be a room sixteen feet long and seventeen feet wide and fifteen feet high for each person; and yet there would be room." But a prepared place implies a prepared people. There is a room in heaven for every one of us, but, unless we live right, that room will be "To Let" through all eternity.

* * *

"God is love." But love is not an effeminate tenderness—a weak, womanish sympathy, that cannot punish the disobedient. God is love, but he is also just, and justice always punishes. There was a time when the terror of the law was preached too much; now the pendulum has swung over to the other extreme—too much love. As a consequence we have much rose-colored religion; a soft, sentimental thing; gaudy rhetoric which means nothing; a religion of words, words—words such as lovers use. We need to-day an aggressive, vigorous, positive Christianity.

* * *

God is bound by the holiness of his nature to punish sin. It is an exercise of power which becomes him as the Moral Governor of the world. There is nothing cruel or vindictive in God to prohibit sin by a law. A law without a penalty is only a dead letter; and the penalty must be such as to deter men from sinning. Is it cruel in God to ordain man with the power of choice? Is God a monster of cruelty because, when I abuse my free agency, he leaves me to suffer the result of my folly?

* * *

If Christ died to save all men, and all men are not saved, is not Christ's work then a failure? Is education a failure because all men are not educated? Christ says: "Ye *will not* come unto me that ye might have life." Christ throws the responsibility of condemnation on men's own consciences. Will God save men against their wills? If men are saved *against* their *wills*, why may they not even rebel against salvation thus forced upon them? If God saves all men, whether they will to be saved or not, he must take away the moral agency with which he has endowed them, and reverse his own nature as revealed in nature and in his Word.

* * *

God is almighty, and therefore he will save everybody if he *can*, and if he can save everybody he *will*. When Christ was groaning in Gethsemane beneath a ponderous load of anguish, he cried out in the deepest agony of his soul: "If it be possible, let this cup pass from me." He prayed the same words three times; yet it appears that the cup did not pass from him; and why may it not be impossible for God to save sinners who hate his law, blaspheme his goodness, reject his grace, scorn his Christ, laugh at his church, hoot at divine mercy, defy divine justice, and persist in rebellion and impenitence to the end? God can no more save such men, because of his very nature, than he can create two mountains without a valley between them.

* * *

Will purgatorial fire fit a soul for heaven? If so, the fundamental Bible principle of divine forgiveness would be done away with. Then why did Christ die? As a matter of fact in human experience, does punishment reform? If so, why is not one trial sufficient? Why are our most hardened criminals men who have been incarcerated over and over again? There have been reformations, but they were brought about through Christian influences. The man given to lust suffers the most excruciating agony, with the full knowledge that his suffering is directly caused by his sin: and, as soon as his paroxysms of suffering are over, he goes again to his transgression and shame. The drunkard suffers again and again all the horrors of the delirium; he is overwhelmed with fears; he believes that the serpents twine themselves about his body, laughingly cuddle in his boots, and fasten their poisonous fangs in his bloated cheeks. He knows that this is the awful penalty of his love for the cup. Aching, rasping, crucifying, damning torture. In hell on earth. Does it reform him? The first thing in the early morning is his cup.

* * *

Time is the only stage of probation. Either here or nowhere are we to prove our fitness for heaven. If men will not hear Christ now, under favorable circumstances, neither will they be persuaded if in some future world Christ should manifest himself to them. If mankind could be made to believe that there was no hell, or that they would be given another chance to repent in the next world, civilization would rush into barbarism. No hell hereafter would mean all hell here. Let a minister in this city rail against hell, and the profane, the drunkard, the libertine and the despiser of things sacred will applaud him, and his name will be heralded notoriously through the press as a reformer; while the men of serious religion, men who pray in their families and closets, who keep the Sabbath holy, and walk humbly with God, will be sad.

I cannot accept Cannon Farrar's gospel of Eternal Hope, because he is not willing to go out of this life trusting his chances of eternal peace to the opportunity of repentance after death. And no man can teach me to believe what he is not willing to practice himself. Of course, you will do as you please; but, for one, I have made up my mind not to take a guess for my dying pillow. Have we not built air castles enough for this life without building any for the next?

XXXV.
That Boy of Yours.

TEACH your boy to be accurate. If he be not taught accuracy in childhood, he will never learn it in his manhood. Teach him to speak accurately on all subjects, and he will scorn to tell a lie.

* * *

Teach your boy the valuable lesson of consideration for the feelings of others. Teach him to disdain revenge. Impress him with this beautiful sentiment: "Write injuries in dust, but kindnesses in marble."

* * *

Let your boy be boyish. A mannish boy, a boy who is a man before his time, is a disagreeable object.

* * *

I never take any stock in the so-called "good boys"— boys who never get into mischief. It is a good thing if they die young, for they generally turn out bad as men.

* * *

Early instill into your boy's mind decision of character. The undecided boy is sure to become a namby-pamby man. He will be as Dryden says:

"Everything by starts and nothing long."

* * *

Teach your boy courtesy. "Manners make the man," says the proverb. True politeness is rapidly becoming in this country one of the "lost arts."

Do not give your boy expensive notions. Bring him up to be simple in his habits and pleasures.

* * *

Teach your boy to look upon labor as a real dignity, and idleness as a disgrace.

* * *

Teach your boy to be open and frank. If he has carelessly broken anything, and takes the full blame upon himself, and makes no excuses about it, don't punish him, but commend him for his honesty, and he will grow up every inch a man.

* * *

Teach your boy to be strictly honest in all his dealings with his brothers and sisters. If he disregard their rights he will grow up to disregard the rights of men. "As the twig is bent the tree inclines."

* * *

Put your boy on his honor. Trust his honor. Nothing will improve his character more. The boy that always requires looking after is in danger.

* * *

Be your boy's companion; treat him as a gentleman; and if such treatment does not make him a gentleman, nothing else will.

* * *

Teach your boy that the best whisky-sling is to sling the bottle or the concealed jug out of the window, and that the best throw of the dice is to throw the dice away.

* * *

Teach your boy not to despise little things. Life is made up of little things. The "little things" in the aggregate make up whatever is great. Look to the littles. If we make the little events of life beautiful and good, then will the whole life be full of beauty and goodness.

Teach your boy to be self-reliant. "Ability and necessity dwell near each other," said Pythagoras. Let your boy learn no other language but this: "You have your own way to make, and it depends upon your own exertion whether you sink or swim, survive or perish." The wisest charity is to help a boy to help himself.

* * *

Teach your boy that there is no such thing as "luck." Good pluck is good luck. Whole-hearted energy crowns men with honors.

* * *

The word "can't" ought not to be found in your boy's vocabulary. Teach him stick-to-it-ness. Don't flinch. Never fly the track. Hold on; hold fast; hold out.

* * *

Teach your boy that the use of tobacco is a filthy, costly and unhealthy habit. The only verse in the Bible that can be quoted in favor of this habit is: "Let him that is filthy be filthy still." The boy with a cigar in his mouth, a swagger in his walk, impudence on his face, a care-for-nothingness in his manner, older than his father (judging from his demeanor), is going too fast. Stop him, father; stop him! The chances are ten to one that in a dishonored grave will soon lie the buried hopes of a father, the joys of a mother's heart, and the pride of sisters fair.

* * *

Teach your boy that if he does not wish to be a nobody, or something much worse than a nobody, he must guard his youth.

* * *

Never permit your boy to associate with your neighbors' badly-managed boys. "He who goes with wolves soon learns to howl." A boy readily copies all that he sees done, good or bad. A boy's temper and habits will be formed on a model of those with whom he associates.

* * *

Above all, bring up that boy of yours in "the nurture and admonition of the Lord." The only way to bring him up in the way of the Lord is for you to walk in that way yourself. Let yours, then, be the religious home, and God's blessings will descend upon it. Your children shall be like "olive plants around your table"—the "heritage of the Lord." It will give to the boy's soul its "perfect flowering," and make it "lustrous in the livery of divine knowledge."

O, parents, if you would sweetly breathe out your last breath on the bosom of Jesus, then neglect not the religious nurture and training of that boy of yours.

XXXVI.

Random Shots.

PRUDERY.

THERE is too much prudery in the world. Prudery is very often nothing more than impurity in a cloak; and "ill-deemers," says the proverb, "are commonly ill-doers." The most immoral thing in the world is some people's respectability.

THE CHRISTIAN ABROAD.

A good many people's religion cannot endure the slight change of climate involved in spending a short time at a summer resort. They seem to say as they go away in the summer: "Good-bye, religion; I'll be back again in the fall."

TALK AND CONVERSATION.

Notwithstanding we are a reading people, there is a great lack of edifying conversation, especially among many young ladies. They can talk, talk, talk, but converse they can't. Why? Because too many read nonsense instead of sense. The ignorance of current events among ladies is deplorable. The man or woman who does not read the daily papers is not worth talking to. The daily newspaper is the mirror of the age.

If half the time and less than half the strength given by many young women to show, fashion, frivolity, crazy-patch work, and to the reading of trashy novels, were devoted to sensible and useful acquisition, what blessings would flow to womankind! It is an offense to an intelligent mind to see a young woman of much pretense, and beauty, and show, and prominence in society, who is unread and uncultivated in those departments about which ordinarily intelligent people are wont to converse.

CARRYING A REVOLVER.

What does any man want with a revolver? Why carry one wherever you go? What has a man with a clear conscience to be afraid of? There is nothing going to hurt you. Be gentlemen, be fair, be honest, be upright, and there will be no reason for the deadly weapon.

EXAGGERATION.

Avoid all exaggeration. Be honest and modest in all your observations. Some men live in a kind of mental telescope, through whose magnifying medium every mouse is turned into an elephant.

LOW-NECKED DRESSES.

The Bible forbids immodesty. Low-necked dresses are in the highest degree immodest. Much of the so-called "full dress" one sees on ladies is only half dress. A really modest man does not know what to do with his eyes. I can never cease wondering how any virtuous and pure-minded female can allow herself to wear one of them in the presence of a large company of people. A man, upon entering a ball-room with a heavy overcoat on, when asked by his wife to explain, said that somebody in the family ought to wear clothing.

TIGHT LACING.

Upon many occasions have I seen women so tightly laced that they actually fought for breath. God so made the heart that it must have room to open and shut, and the lungs must have room to be filled with air. To give them room, and keep anything from pressing against them, God has built around them a bone fence. When the waist is tightly laced the ribs are pressed in upon the heart and lungs, and neither of them has room to do its work properly. If they could speak for themselves, what a terrible outcry the poor, suffering hearts and lungs would make! It is astonishing how many women are dissatisfied with the way the Lord made them.

HORSE-RACING.

I don't believe that the cultivation of a horse's speed is a sin. If the Lord made fast horses, it was to have them go fast. But the evil begins when the betting begins—when fast horses make fast men. Gambling is accursed of God. Upon the brow of every pool-seller I would write the unmistakable word "Swindler." I know of many men and women who bet on horses last summer, and I do not know of one who won. I am glad of it. I hope it may so discourage them that they may quit. If a man gain he is apt to go right on to hell.

ILL TEMPER.

Religion should influence our temper. If a man be as jealous, passionate, revengeful, huffy, sullen, morose, sour and moody after his conversion as before it, what is he converted from or to? The Christian should cherish like an apple of gold a bright, sunny, cheerful temper and disposition.

TRUE RELIGION.

Be good, and do the most good that you can now and here, and help others to be and do the same. Do good with what you have, or it will do you no good. Be not simply good; be good for something. Some of you are so good that you are good for nothing.

BUSYBODIES.

The man who minds his own business has his hands full. If you have no business, then make it your business to leave the business of others alone. They who know most about other people's business generally fail in their own. Some people are so busy meddling with other people's business, and so seldom minding their own, that I would not be at all surprised, at the general resurrection, to find them getting out of somebody else's grave.

TRUE LIVING.

John the Baptist preached about eighteen months. But he had the courage of his convictions; he did his duty, and his glory streams down the ages and floods the whole earth. He died at the age of thirty-three years, and yet the angel said he should be "great in the sight of the Lord." We may not preach long, but let us preach courageously. We may die young, but we can leave behind us foot-prints on the sands of time, reminding others that they, too, can make their lives sublime.

"We live in deeds, not years; in thoughts, not breaths;
In feelings, not in figures on a dial.
We should count time by heart-throbs. He most lives
Who thinks most, feels the noblest, acts the best;
And he whose heart beats quickest lives the longest—
Lives in one hour more than in years do some
Whose fat blood sleeps as it slips along their veins."

THE SENSITIVE MAN.

The most troublesome man in the church is not the rudely outspoken one; nor yet the chronic grumbler and objector; nor yet the perpetual critic and fault-finder; nor yet the church-gossip; bad as they are, they are not so bad as the man who applies every thoughtless remark, every word and deed that is capable of inappreciable interpretation to himself, and who is continually being hurt, offended and insulted. You can scarcely crook your finger without giving him offense. He is always on the lookout for slights and insults, and takes them when they are neither intended nor given. The least little thing throws him off his guard into a whirlwind of passion, and he threatens to leave the church. Don't be easily provoked. Keep cool. Be slow to take offense. "Soon fire—soon ashes." Forgive injuries. Remember, that "To err is human; to forgive divine." Be merciful, as you expect God to be merciful to you. Show that clemency to all men that you expect Christ to show to you.

TABLE PRAYER.

Table prayer is a plain, Christian duty. Our Lord always gave thanks before eating. So did the early Christians. So should we. It is one mark of a Christian family. It is confessing Christ before men. It is an easy duty. Who cannot say: "Dear Father. we thank thee for our daily bread, and pray thee bless it to our use."

A CURE FOR ANGER.

It is said of Julius Cæsar that, when provoked, he used to repeat the whole Roman alphabet before he suffered himself to speak. Thomas Jefferson said: "When angry, count ten before you speak; if very angry, a hundred." Solomon said: "He that is slow to wrath is of great understanding, but he that is hasty of spirit exalteth folly."

A GOOD RULE FOR THE MARRIED.

Matthew Henry tells of a couple who were both passionate naturally, but who lived very happily together by simply observing this rule: *never to be both angry at the same time.* Take turn about.

OBJECTORS.

A man, upon making application for membership in an active church, being asked what he could do, said: "Well, I am good on objections. If anything is proposed, I can object to it." Our churches are full of such men and women, who, too lazy to do any work, simply ease their consciences by objecting.

Two laborers were trying to place a stone in position on the foundation-wall of a new building. A crowd was standing around looking on, and each one offering his criticisms and counsel freely and loudly, but not one lifting so much as a finger to help. "That reminds me of church work," said one passer-by to another. "Why?" asked his friend. "Because," was the reply, "two men are doing the work and the rest are doing the talking." Work or be still.

AFFECTATION.

About the most painful thing to listen to is an affected young lady—drawling, and lisping, and chopping, and clipping her words. If she could only see herself as others see her, she would then know what a simpleton she makes of herself. Some one has said: "Affectation is a greater enemy to the face than small-pox."

THE EDUCATION OF WOMAN.

The education of woman involves issues of the most serious and far-reaching kind; for, as some one has said: "When you educate a woman, you educate a race." There are men who spend thousands of dollars in the education of their boys (and often on five-dollar boys), who spend little, if anything, in the education of their daughters. But such a narrow-minded, squeezing, wrenching, grasping, scraping, clutching and covetous old sinner can never expect to become my father-in-law.

LITTLE BAD HABITS.

Take care of your *little* bad habits. Little ones are only great ones condensed into small forms, as the serpent in the egg, the explosion in the cold powder. The embankment of earth, so long as it is entire, can hold in its strong embrace the swelling floods of a mighty river. But let the destroyer take a little instrument and make a small opening. The opening becomes larger and larger, until a foaming torrent comes roaring through the breach, sweeps over fertile plains and buries whole cities. So a little habit will grow and grow, and when the rains descend and the floods rise and the winds blow, your character will be swept away.

> "A little theft, a small deceit,
>   Too often leads to more;
> 'Tis hard at first, but tempts the feet
>   As through an open door.
> Just as the broadest rivers run
>   From small and distant springs,
> The greatest crimes that men have done
>   Have grown from little things."

FRESH AIR.

Man needs plenty of fresh air. Close houses, close stores and close factories mean impure air. Without airy houses, stores, shops and factories, nature cannot do the work she is striving to do. I do not wonder that so many people's health fails, their strength leaves them, and their very minds become enfeebled. Sleep in the best and airiest room. Breathing vitiated atmosphere, especially in sleep, destroys muscular strength.

LOVE IS NOT ALL.

Love is not all. It is quite possible to love one wholly unworthy of you. It does not follow that because two are uncomfortable apart they will be happy together.

PARENTAL INDULGENCE.

Absalom's father, David, spared the rod and spoiled the boy. How many such wrecks as Absalom lie stranded on the beach of time! They were shattered on the same rock—parental indulgence. O, parents, will you not forestall these unavailing lamentations, these moans of blasted hopes and broken hearts, that are darkening and burdening the earth? Tell your children exactly what to do, and then make them do it. "Correct thy son, and he shall give thee rest." "Chasten thy son while there is hope." Judicious, steadfast authority exalts the parent, and makes his love inestimable.

SUNLIGHT.

Man is just like a plant: it is only in the sunlight he can live. Cook or bake yourself thoroughly in the sun every day. Let your children bask in the sunshine. If you let the sun shine into your houses the carpets may lose some of their rich, deep color; but as this lost color will pass into the cheeks and lips of your children, you need not mourn the faded carpets. I would rather have pale carpets than pale people. An Italian proverb says: "Where the sun does not come in the doctor does."

MONOPOLIES.

By a monopoly I mean rich men buying up all competitors and crushing them out of existence; getting control of some commodity; crushing out all fair competition, which is the life of trade, and dictating the price. Any set of men who, by any combination or action, compel us to pay more than the nominal prices for what we eat and drink and wear, are guilty of highway robbery. The swindling of these wholesale robbers is called percentage; their wrong-heartedness, long-headedness; their duplicity, shrewdness.

GAMBLING.

Gambling is a poor business. Every gambler sooner or later goes to the dogs. It is an unhappy business. The gloomiest set of men in the world are your betting men. They are always on the edge of a precipice; they are in perpetual danger of being reduced to beggary. It is an immoral business. When rogue meets rogue, then comes the tug of scoundrelism.

DON'T.

Don't tell everything you hear. Don't blister your tongue with backbiting. Don't be the devil's bellows to blow up the fire of strife in the community. Either cut off a bit of your tongue or season it with the salt of grace. Be quick at work and slow at talk. Think of your own faults ere other people's faults you tell. "People who live in glass houses should never throw stones."

MARRYING FOR MONEY.

Do not make matrimony simply a *matter of money*. There is nothing objectionable in a man if, along with worth, he has money. But—

> "In many a marriage made for gold,
> The bride is bought and the bridegroom sold."

Though Cupid is said to be blind, he is a far better guide than the rules of arithmetic. Love is the golden chord in marriage. What false ideas of happiness we have! When John Jacob Astor was told that he must be a very happy man, being so rich, he said: "Why, would you take care of my property for your board and clothes? That's all I get paid." Have a fortune *in* your husband, which is far better than to have one with your husband. It is better to have a *man* without money, than money without a *man*.

FALSE MEASURES.

There is a great deal of stealing nowadays by short weights and measures. This sin is lamentably common. The Sealer of Weights and Measures showed that in one year, in one of our large cities, nearly seven thousand weights and measures were found incorrect. When all the measures get to be the same size you may look out for the millennium. Give some of our merchants the right to sell out the Delaware river by the quart and they would cheat you in the measurement.

TRUST NOT APPEARANCES.

In the decision of the sacred question of marriage, be not influenced by appearances. The maintaining of appearances is the great snare and evil of our times. Never judge a man by the coat he wears. It may be borrowed or unpaid for. Remember that the deepest rascals are often the finest clothed and smoothest tongued. With what great care you purchase a good dress! How you hold it up to the light, that you may see every shade and detect any defect! Be not less considerate in that important event which is to link your life and destiny with another. Be satisfied with nothing but sober reality.

MARRY THE MAN.

Don't marry because somebody asks you to marry. Marry *the* man, not any man. Look before you leap. Go slow. Think where you are going. As Davy Crockett said: "*Be sure you are right, then go ahead.*" Remember that a father's home and a mother's counsel, and the society of brothers and sisters are affections that last, while those of many a young man wane in the honey-moon.

Nothing so much causes ill-assorted marriages and mischievous results as making "old maid" a term of reproach. Many girls have been hurled into matrimony by the dread of being so stigmatized, and have repented the step to their dying day. Many women can give more honorable reasons for living outside the temple of Hymen than their foolish sisters can for having rushed in. Some have never found their other selves. Providential circumstances may have prevented the junction of these selves; and is not a life of loneliness more honorable than a loveless marriage? Is not single blessedness preferable to double cursedness?

There are many women who laid down their hopes of wedded bliss for the sake of accomplishing some good. In such cases singleness is an honorable estate. There is a work for woman in the world, married or single, as wife, mother, sister, daughter or friend.

A WARNING.

I warn you, young man, against the gossiping gad-about. She will drive you mad. A man said to his wife: "Double up your whip." He meant keep your tongue quiet. It must be a terrible thing to be living with a whip that is always lashing you. A blind man, having a shrew for a wife, was told by one of his friends that she was a rose. He replied: "I do not doubt it, sir, for I feel the thorns daily." There is nothing grander than a bright and contented disposition.

WHAT GIRLS SHOULD KNOW.

A good wife must have mental attractiveness. I do not say that she must be well versed in classic lore and polite literature, but she must have that common intelligence, fit for every-day use, which is absolutely essential to make her intercourse with society pleasing to herself and agreeable to others. And the girl who is ignorant in these days generally has but two excuses for her ignorance: she was either lazy, or crazy after the boys. A good wife must at least know enough of physiology to appreciate the importance of cleanliness of person and in the house. A carelessly dressed, slatternly and untidy woman cannot long keep her place on the throne of her husband's life. From a lazy, slovenly woman may heaven deliver you! The devil tempts everybody, but a slovenly woman tempts the devil. Young man, look out where you are going! A lazy girl will make a lazy wife, just as sure as a crooked sapling will make a crooked tree. A good wife should know enough of arithmetic to check the accounts of merchants and marketmen, and reckon the amount saved by paying cash. The reason why so many people get along so miserably in life, and have so many obstacles to surmount, is because they have no knowledge of arithmetic.

A WISE CHOICE.

A young man who had long been absent called upon two beautiful young ladies of his acquaintance. One came quickly to meet him in the neat, yet not precise attire in which she was performing her household duties. The other, after a lapse of half an hour, made her stately entrance in all the primness of starch and ribbons, with which, on the announcement of his entrance, she had hastened to bedeck herself. The young man, who had long been hesitating as to his choice between the two, now hesitated no longer. The cordiality with which the first hastened to greet him, and the charming carelessness of her attire, entirely won his heart. She is now his wife. He was a sensible man. Take warning from this. Never be afraid to see a friend because you are in your working gown. No true gentleman will think less of you because he finds you in the performance of your duty, and he will think all the more of you if you are not ashamed to let it be known. O, young ladies, love home! Of that realm you are the queens. Fit yourselves to fulfill its divine prerogatives; for in the home is embosomed God's own trust, the glory of the state, the hope of the church, and the destiny of the world. Oh, the illimitableness of which you are capable! Love home! Prize its duties! Live for it, and you will secure to yourselves such testimony as Abraham Lincoln proudly bore to his mother, when he said: "All I am, my mother made me;" and above all, you will secure the approval of God.

GIRLS' EXTRAVAGANCE.

The extravagance of girls prevents thousands of young men from marrying. Thousands of young men in this city, already engaged, are putting off marriage from year to year until they can make enough to support their wives. Too many young women want to begin where their parents left off. Too many young men are too proud themselves to commence married life in a quiet, economical way. If they cannot continue their private luxuries and support their wives in style, they put off marriage. Begin as your fathers began, and work up, save up, grow up. This is the only way to get up. Young ladies and gentlemen, I beseech you be true to the best feelings of your hearts, careless about what the world will say, and pure and happy Christian homes will be more abundant.

FLIRTING.

Flirting is trifling with the most sacred and serious relations of human life. Marriage can never be esteemed if courtship be made a round of low frolic and fun. Let all your dealings with women be frank, honest and noble. Be this your motto: *I will treat every woman I meet as I would wish another man to treat my innocent, confiding sister.*

THE NOVEL.

I do not wage war indiscriminately against the novel, for there are pure, good novels. The world owes a debt of obligation to such fictitious writers as Hawthorne, Marion Harland, Walter Scott, Charles Kingsley, Thackeray, Dickens, Roe, Howells and others, whose names easily occur to you; and this debt of obligation can only be paid by reading their works. They will elevate, purify and ennoble mankind. The popular novel may be described in Pollok's words:

> "A novel is a book
> Crammed full of poisonous error, blacking every page;
> And oftener still of trifling, second-hand
> Remark, and old, diseased, putrid thought.
> And miserable incident at war
> With nature; with itself and truth at war:
> Yet charming still the greedy reader on,
> Till done, he tries to recollect his thought,
> And nothing finds but dreaming emptiness."

It may be written in eloquent and polished style, vivid in its portraiture, but it is damnable in its influence. Avoid all books which present false pictures of human life. They are dangerous! Stand aloof!

AN ILLOGICAL CRITICISM.

The minister who preaches in the pulpit like an angel and lives in the world like a devil is the guiltiest man that the sun shines upon. But the world is too rigorous and exacting. Damaging as the criticism is, that the preacher does not live up to what he preaches, it is also illogical, because, as a preacher, it is his duty to say the best things. It is his duty as a man to live up to them.

Would it not be absurd if he recommended only what he lived—a limited purity, a qualified faith—because he felt he could rise no higher himself? In the pulpit the preacher is bound to take the highest possible ground; hence it is obvious that his faults, which are inevitable, should be kept out of sight of his hearers.

SNOBBERY.

There is a large class of people in this country who imitate English life. There is an alarming tendency to depreciate American life. Many Americans look across the ocean for their example. This raging Anglo-mania reaches everything; no matter how ugly, it must be in affectation of the English. We go wild over the aristocratic swells who tramp through our country, accept our hospitality, and, like Matthew Arnold and others, upon their return home, fill the English press with tirades on American life. The average Englishman, who has always lived on a narrow island, has not breadth of mind enough to grasp American greatness. America is ahead of England in everything that makes a nation great. Let there be no more affecting English manners. Let Americans stand by their nativity!

COMMON-SENSE EDUCATION.

Artemus Ward once said he "tried to do too much and did it." That is just the weak point in our schools and colleges: much is done, but not enough done thoroughly and well. While a little knowledge may be a dangerous thing, too much is too much. Many minds are so rounded and polished by education as not to be energetic in any one faculty; so symmetrical as to have no point; while other men not thus trained are led to efforts that render them at last far more learned and better educated than the polished and easy-going graduate who has just knowledge enough to prevent consciousness of his ignorance. The end of life is *to be* and *do*, not to read and brood over what men have been and done. Shakespeare refers to this exquisite cultivation when he speaks of "the native hue of resolution being sicklied o'er with the pale cast of thought."

Pope says truly: "Some men are too refined for action." The vast majority of our most successful men are not polished scholars. This tends to show what is too commonly forgotten in modern plans of education: that it is far better to have the mind well disciplined than richly stored, strong rather than full. Good common sense—the power of adaptation to circumstances, the secret of being alive to what is going on around one, of knowing what the people want, and of saying and doing the right thing at the right time and place, is the crown of faculties.

A TRADE.

It is a rule in the imperial family of Germany that every young man shall acquire a trade, going through a regular apprenticeship till he is able to do good, fair journey work. This is because kingdoms are subject to vicissitudes, and it is deemed necessary to a manly independence that the heir-apparent or a prince of the blood should be conscious of ability to make his own way in the world, if needs be. This is an honorable custom, worthy of imitation. Franklin says: "He that hath a trade, hath an estate." Work, however looked down upon by people who cannot perform it, is an honorable thing; it may not be very profitable, but honorable it always is; there's nothing to be ashamed of in it. The man who has reason to be ashamed is the man who does nothing. Let the dandy whose conceit greatly exceeds his brains be ashamed of his kid gloves, but never let a man who works be ashamed of his hard hands.

COMING TO TOWN.

Young man, be sure you can better yourself in the city before you leave your comfortable home or place in the country. The chances are, if you come to the city, you will wish yourself back again in the country before the year is over. It is hard for the country boy to do well in the city now, as our cities are overcrowded. The greatest slave on earth is the average city clerk. With proper care and effort, country life can be made as enjoyable and profitable as city life. Spend in the country towns and villages the same amount for concerts, lectures, etc., that you would if you came to the city, and you will have almost equal advantages. Farmers should settle in colonies. Let them live in villages. It is a pleasure to go a mile or two to work. The isolation of American farm life is its curse.

BE PROGRESSIVE.

Advance with the advancement of the times, and advance in the front ranks. Don't get set in your ways. Be open to new ideas. Be enterprising, and you will succeed. The business houses which follow the old methods go to the wall. Let the next thing always be something else. It is true that if you are original and enterprising you will be opposed. But opposition will prevent dull times, and criticism is the whetstone by which a genuine man is polished and sharpened. People have opposed everything new. The inventor of the umbrella was stigmatized for interrupting the designs of Providence with regard to the rainy weather; for when the showers fell it was evident God meant that men should get wet. The man who brought that balm into the world, anæsthetics, was also stigmatized. By the aid of this, the most violent surgical operation can be performed, while pain is banished into dreamland. The design of Providence, it was claimed, was that, if a man's limb must be amputated, it should ache, and the inventor frustrated that design. Vaccination was stigmatized as the work of the devil; because disease is, by its nature, made contagious by God, and man should not interfere with God's doing. It was meddling with Providence. That kind of logic has always existed in the world; it exists still. So don't be afraid of criticism. Advance! If you can do anything better to-day than it was done yesterday, do it, regardless of what your father or grandfather did, for they and their methods have passed away. Be alive; be original; be enterprising. Go forward. Don't stand still. The perfectly satisfied man and the clam are first cousins.

RELIGION IN BUSINESS.

It matters not how a man may say his prayers, if he depart from the path of strict rectitude in business his religion is worthless. If his Christianity be not good behind the counter, if it will not bar out falsehood, and personal greed, and sharp practice, and low cunning, it is a sham. "Without works your faith is dead." That is, if you don't live during the week what you profess on Sunday, your religion is a humbug. Carry your religion with you into every-day life. Let your religion be a reality. Bring it down from the clouds. Suffuse all your actions with holy principles.

ONE COVENANT.

The covenant of works and of grace are one. It was ordained in Christ of God from the foundation of the world. The covenant of grace was the original covenant, made not after the failure of the Edenic transaction, but existing prior to its inauguration, and existing prior to the creation of man—from the beginning, from eternity. The covenant of Christ is the original policy of the original government. Christ was away back, from the very beginning of the world, saving the world. Christ is *"Alpha and Omega—the first and the last."* He is *"the same yesterday, to-day and forever."* *"The Lamb slain from the foundation of the world."*

ORIGINAL SIN.

We do not teach that we are guilty of Adam's sin, or responsible for his act in the sense of being criminal, but that we have inherited from Adam a depraved nature; we have lost original righteousness. Our corrupt nature is called original sin, because it is the nature of sin, because it comes from the first parents, because it is the source of all other sins in the individual, and to distinguish it from actual sin. We have inherited from Adam a depraved nature. Now what are the facts in the case? Does not the babe suffer? Is not suffering the natural consequence of sin? Do we not see that the very first tendency in children is to disobey? Do they not naturally incline to the wrong? Why so? Do not men inherit a diseased moral nature? Do not men willfully disobey the moral law, and alienate themselves from God? Sin is born in the child as surely as fire is in the flint; it only waits to be brought out and manifested. Surely no one can deny actual sin. Now, did you ever see a tree growing without a root?

Our nature is depraved. Contrasted with the character of God, man is unholy, unclean, impure, as demonstrated by the records and by the facts of daily life. Man is the very opposite of what he should be and must be before he can hope to find that heavenly way which leads unto eternal life. Man, in order to bring himself into sympathy with God, must be changed into the moral likeness of God, so that there can be some basis for union and some ground for fellowship; for "what concord hath light with darkness?" Man must begin life anew, on different principles, with new convictions, affections, resolves, inspiring a new manner and course of life. This must be the result of a higher power operating upon him. If you ask: "What power hath God over me?" I respond, he has as much power over you as the man you employ to graft your trees has over those trees. Man can take a tree that bears this year sour apples and make it bear, a few years from now, sweet ones. Is not God able to do as much with your heart as that man is with the trees you never made, but only bought? If man can change the tree, cannot God change you? Try it, my friend. Ask him in faith to graft you with a new order of life, and your life will henceforth be sweet.

"THE ELECT."

How may you know that you are among "the elect?" If you choose to come to God, he has solemnly declared: "*Him that cometh unto me I will in no wise cast out.*" The question is: Come or not come? Choose or not choose? When you decide the question and come, then you settle the matter of your election; by obeying the divine command you make "your calling and *election* sure." The eternal decrees of God are, that the farmer shall have a crop if he do his part—plow and sow. The farmer knows this, and he knows that he will not have a harvest unless he sows the seed. The decrees of God are made conditional on his doing. So in the matter of salvation: God has "elected" that your soul will or will not be saved, and he tells you that you will be saved if you come to Christ, and will not be saved if you do not come to Christ. "*Whosoever will may come.*" The whosoever will are the elect; the whosoever won't are the non-elect. Don't tease yourselves with useless inquiries, and perplex yourselves with the secret counsels of God; attend to your plain duties. repent and believe, and your salvation will be sure.

THE MAIN THING.

Do not allow the technicalities of religion to stop your salvation. There are men who are all the time asking questions, and making discussion the refuge of their guilt. They debate in order that they may not decide. They have studied redemption, but not the Redeemer; Christianity. but not Christ. Instead of discussing whether the serpent in Eden was figurative or literal, or the wars of the Jews, and Jonah, or troubling yourself about the difficulties suggested by the book of *Revelation*, look to Christ; believe on him, and take him as your master and model, and you will not be slow to find out that "all Scripture is given by inspiration of God." You may never have all your difficulties solved, or all your objections met, but you may plant your feet upon the Rock of Ages. The great point with you is not this or that doctrine; not whether you agree or disagree with evangelical Christians. The great point is this: Are you at peace with God? Do you think and feel as he wishes you to feel? Is your soul, is your conscience, is your conduct in harmony with him? *How do you stand before God?* I leave the level of faith, and come to that of practice and conduct. Love and repentance first; theology second.

THE ATONEMENT.

Christ bore human sin as a representative of man before the divine law—a *sacrifice for sin*, a *substitute for man*, and a *satisfaction* to law. Christ, the Lord himself, suffered on account of the broken law, in order that the majesty of the law might be honored to the full. Some time ago one of our judges was called upon to try a prisoner who had been his companion in early youth. It was a crime for which the penalty was a heavy fine. The judge did not diminish the fine, but fined the prisoner to the full. Some who knew his former relation to the offender thought him somewhat unkind thus to carry out the law, while others praised his impartiality. All were surprised when the judge quitted the bench and himself paid every farthing of the penalty. He had shown his respect for the law and his good-will to the man who had broken it; he exacted the penalty, but paid it himself. That is just what God has done in the person of his Son, Jesus Christ our Lord; and for the sake of Christ's righteousness we shall be treated as righteous, being made righteous by his grace. Some years ago a man of high standing married an Indian girl in one of our Western cities, for he saw in her the capabilities of noble womanhood. She was educated, and subsequently moved in the highest circles of society, for the sake of her husband, who was held in the highest esteem. The doctrine that God treats sinners with favor for the sake of his Son finds many analogies even in human society.

THE FAITHFUL SERVANT GIRLS.

Who has not heard early on Sunday mornings the tramp, tramp, tramp of people with a hard day's work before them, hastening to the Catholic church, with prayer-book in hand? No people deserve more praise than the poor servant girls. Though worked so hard, while we are yet asleep, they go to their church and lay a goodly portion of their earnings upon her altars. Can God refuse their sacrifice? They put us to shame. Would to God Protestants were as faithful!

THE JEW.

The Irishman who whipped the Jew, when asked why he did so, replied: "That man is a Jew." "Well, what of that?" "The Jews," replied the Irishman, "killed Christ." "Yes; but that was more than 1800 years ago." "Well, never mind," said the Irishman; "I only heard of it to-day." Many of us seem to be as ignorant. Shall the deed of his ancestors be laid against the Jew and his descendants down to the sixtieth generation? Were those ancestors guilty of crucifying the Messiah? Would they have put Jesus Christ to death had they believed him to be the Messiah? Hear Paul: "Which none of the princes of the world knew; for, had they known it, they would not have crucified the Lord of Glory." Listen to Jesus on the cross: "Father, forgive them, for they know not what they do." Is it not time that we forgive and forget what Christ forgave 1800 years ago? The Jew rejects Christ, but believes in the Messiah. Who shall say now that his "faith," like Abraham's, shall not be accounted unto him for righteousness? With all the rough handling the world has given the Jew, it is wonderful that he has no more faults. For, as Shakespeare made Shylock to say: "He hath disgraced me, and hindered me of half a million, laughed at my losses, mocked at my gains, scorned my nation, thwarted my bargains, cooled my friends, heated my enemies—and what's his reason? I am a Jew. Hath not a Jew eyes? Hath not a Jew hands, organs, dimensions, senses, affections, passions? Is he not fed with the same food, hurt with the same weapon, subject to the same diseases, healed by the same means, warmed and cooled by the same winter and summer as a Christian is? If you prick us do we not bleed? If you tickle us do we not laugh? If you poison us do we not die? and if you wrong us shall we not revenge?" It is high time that we should lay aside all bigotry. We are all children of a common Father.

TIME.

Dr. Young truly said: "The man is yet unborn who truly weighs an hour." Some one records having seen the following notice: "Lost! somewhere between sunrise and sunset, two golden hours, each set with sixty diamond minutes. No reward is offered for their recovery, for they are lost forever!" The day that ends with the setting sun will never come back. Franklin asks: "Dost thou love life? Then do not squander time, for that is the stuff life is made of." Fill each day and every hour with something to do.

BENEVOLENCE.

Selfishness is ugly. How beautiful woman appears on errands of mercy. I confess I always feel as if I should bow in reverence and take off my hat whenever I pass the Sisters of Charity. Their black garments should be exchanged for the white robes of heaven, for they seem so godlike. But we, too, have our sisters of charity, who practically follow Him who "went about doing good." A large heart of charity is a beautiful thing. Everybody predicts a beautiful life from a good-doing young woman.

ENVY.

Envy, like Milton's fiend, sees undelighted all delight. Hannah Moore calls envy "the ugliest fiend of hell," and

Spenser declares: "Of all the passions in the mind, thou vilest art."

And what produces envy? The excellence of another. Envy is, then, only the acknowledgment of inferiority—the homage paid to excellence. A man that makes a character makes enemies. A radiant genius calls forth swarms of biting, stinging insects, just as the sunshine awakens the world of flies. "I don't like you," said the snow-flake to the snow-bird. "Why don't you like me?" said the snow-bird. "Oh," said the snow-flake, "I'm going down and you are going up."

PURITY.

Purity precedes all spiritual attainment and progress. It is the letter A in the moral alphabet. However beautiful your face, and varied your attainments, and charming your social qualities, you are nothing without purity—only tinkling cymbals. An impure woman is an awful sight. She outrages all just ideas of womanhood, all proper conceptions of true beauty. A French author says: "Beauty unaccompanied by virtue is a flower without perfume." She is not beautiful, however complete on the outside, who is faulty and unsightly within.

CHRIST'S TEXT-BOOK.

Christ's text-book was every-day life. He spoke up to the times. He did not read off any dry theological abstractions. He spoke to the men who lived around him doing all kinds of mischief. We find him in the market places, in the streets where the people congregate. We find him in all the activities of life. He lived in an age of corruption, and he never shut his mouth concerning it. He never used language of diplomacy, of expediency, of policy. He called everything by its right name.

GETTING ON IN THE WORLD.

Let us pass along the streets of beauty, comfort and wealth. These people who live here have come up mostly from the multitude. Here we see the rewards of industry, economy and perseverance. You say they were lucky. I say they were plucky.

But how did they get on? By never getting off—on sprees—and spending their time in idleness. They cultivated the higher attributes of manhood; for brain power always takes the precedence of brute force. Instead of spending their time in clamoring for higher wages and fewer hours work per day, they devoted their time to learning how to do better work, which so often insures that prosperity which clamor and complaining never win. It is the sheerest nonsense and a sad waste of time for the laboring men to make faces at the capitalists. The one is dependent upon the other. How shall we solve this problem? Let every man start out and begin to be a capitalist himself, and let him make the best bargain he can for himself. Level up, boys; level up, straighten up, reach up, grow up, save up; this is the only way you can get up and overshadow the men who abuse their power.

PRAYER.

Let prayer be the fixed habit of your life. It is the beaten path to greatness. Nothing under heaven gives men such majesty of resources, and such a vision into the unseen and imperishable, as the cry of the heart in devout, believing prayer. Daniel, on his knees with his window opened toward Jerusalem, was greater than when administering the affairs of the empire. Luther was more a champion of liberty and truth at the mercy seat than when nailing his theses to the church-door in Wittenberg, or when standing in lone grandeur before the royal ecclesiastical tribunal at Worms. Newton was more a giant when telling his wants to God than when pursuing his bright way through the heavens. Washington prayed, and he never fought such battles as when bowed before God in the bush or under the covering of his tent. Abraham Lincoln was a greater man on his knees before God, imploring him to drive Lee out of Pennsylvania, than when he signed the emancipation proclamation. When, on the death of William IV. of England, June 20, 1837, Victoria, but eighteen years and seven days old, was awakened in the night, and told by the Prelate that the throne of the United Kingdom of Great Britain and Ireland was hers, the first thing she said was: "I ask your prayers," and then and there they knelt down and prayed. Since that time all the governments of Europe have been worn out or fearfully shaken, but hers stands as firm as it did the day she ascended it; and wherever, the world over, her name is pronounced, every Englishman feels like taking of his hat and shouting: "*God save the Queen!*" Let the light and power from the throne of God fall on every step of your career, and you will be winners in the race of life.

THE CHEAP SYSTEM.

To many people a thing that is cheap has a charming attractiveness. The cheap house is praised to the skies. I have a holy hatred for the word "cheap." It means cheap labor and dishonest work. It is a blood-stained tyrant. Think how cheap things become cheap, and you will be left comfortless; your solace will become your sorrow. The bold figures in our windows, advertising cheap things, ought to be written with blood, and in God's sight are. How are prices forced down? By the wages of the workers being forced back. The purchaser says:

"It is cheap." The workingwoman says: "It is death." God only knows how much buying on the cheap is responsible for fallen virtue. What is good is cheap at a good price. What is cheap is too dear at any price. What you can buy "dirt cheap" usually *is* dirt. And your advertised "*great bargains*" are usually *great sells*.

DECISION OF CHARACTER.

Be decided. Know you are right, and then sail right on. Have the courage to say "No." Be brave for the right. Dare to be true. Dare to stand alone. God will smite every peril before you, and close every mouth that would threaten or defame you.

> "Let the road be long and dreary,
> And its ending out of sight:
> Foot it bravely, never weary,
> Trust in God, and do the right."

YOUNG MAN, BEWARE!

Young man, I warn you against the man who lives fast, knows the town, is up to all the dodges of licentious villainy, rolls all the vile and sensual gossip under his tongue, who boasts of the "wild oats" he is sowing, and who takes a fiendish delight in undermining the principle and ridiculing the scruples of the uninitiated. Cut such a companion off and cast him from you. Forsake that saloon, give up that club, frequent no longer that convivial meeting which breaks up after the midnight hour, and the members of which, inflamed with strong drink and licentious stories and songs, go madly to seek the gratification of their fevered and raging lusts. "Come out from among them and be separate." It is better that you should go companionless to heaven, than that with these sons of Belial you should be cast into hell.

FANCY PICTURES.

It is quite common for young men, and older men, too, who ought to have better sense, to carry pictures of cigarette girls, actresses, etc. Show me what kind of pictures a man likes to look at, and I will tell you what kind of a man he is. Unclean pictures are doing a mighty work for death. Young man, carry *your mother's picture* with you. Bind it to your bosom, and when tempted to do some evil, or to go to some place of evil concourse, consult that silent monitor. Draw forth and look upon that face! Oh, with what tremendous, resistless eloquence it would warn, plead and entreat you to keep back from all evil, and inspire you to ascend to the realities of eternity.

TRUST NOT TOO FAR.

It is wise not to trust your best friend too far, for he may some day be your enemy. Many who have trusted their friends too far, could have cried out with Queen Elizabeth: "In trust have I found treason;" or with Julius Cæsar, when stabbed by Brutus: "And thou also, Brutus!" Cæsar received twenty wounds, mostly at the hands of those whose lives he had spared.

COMPANIONSHIP WITH FOOLS.

Solomon says: "A companion of fools shall be destroyed." A wise and good teacher once refused to let his son and daughter go into what he considered unsafe company when they were quite grown up. The daughter accused her father of underestimating their development into manhood and womanhood. To convince her of her mistake and the pernicious effects of associating with the bad, the father gave her a dead coal of fire, and requested her to handle it. Her white hands were soon soiled, and she said to her father: "We cannot be too careful in handling coals." "Yes, truly," said her father; "you see, my child, that coal, even if it do not burn, it blackens. So it is with the company of the vicious." There is nothing in which the young ought to be more careful than in selecting their company.

It is impossible to take coals of fire in our bosom and not be burned. Neither can we associate with the low and vulgar without becoming low and vulgar ourselves. The ancient Pythagoras, before he admitted any one into his school, made inquiry as to who his associates had been, rightly judging that those who had been careless about their companionships were not likely to derive much benefit from his instruction.

Associate with the sinful as little as possible. You may mean to purify them, but the chances are that you will be corrupted. A story is told of two parrots that lived near to each other. One was accustomed to sing hymns, while the other was addicted to swearing. The owner of the latter obtained permission for it to associate with the former, in the hope that its bad habit would be corrected; but the opposite result followed, for both learned to swear alike.

Petrarch says: "Let no man deceive himself by thinking that the contagions of the soul are less than those of the body. They are yet greater: they sink deeper and come on more unsuspectedly."

Nothing is truer than that men and women will be judged by the company they keep. "Birds of a feather flock together." And, as the Germans say: "*Mitgefangen, mitgehangen.*"

SILENCE.

A German proverb says: "Speech is silver; silence is gold." Carlyle says: "Silence is deep as eternity; speech is shallow as time." Denouncing the vapid verbiage of shallow praters, he again exclaims: "Even triviality and imbecility, that can be silent, how respectable are they in comparison!" Cato says: "I think the first virtue is to restrain the tongue; he approaches nearest the gods who knows how to be silent, even though he is in the right." He who knows when to keep his tongue still has a wise head. Yet, as some one has said: "Silence is just as far from being wisdom as the rattle of an empty wagon is from being music." Many a man passes for wise simply because he is too big a fool to talk.

"PAY AS YOU GO."

John Randolph's favorite maxim is a good one—"Pay as you go." If you cannot pay, do not go. There are men in every community who live by a form of petty thieving—making small loans and incurring small bills which they never pay. Debt is a foe to a man's honesty. Live this month on what you earned last month, not on what you are going to earn next month.

KEEP THE CHILDREN AT SCHOOL.

What a pity that so many children are taken out of school just when they are beginning to learn. Boys and girls taken out of school and cooped up in stores, shops and factories, are not only mentally impoverished, but physically ruined, and that too for a miserable pittance. It is a false economy to make children earn their bread too soon. While at school, the history, geography, grammar, physiology and natural philosophy they learn constitute the knowledge that will be their capital when they enter on the business of life. Intelligent workmen are cheaper at higher wages than the uneducated. Give your children the best education you possibly can.

Even if they should not live to profit by their education, and should disappoint all your hopes, still you will have the consciousness of having discharged your duty to them; of having done all in your power to make them what God willed they should be—*men and women.*

TRUE BLUE BLOOD.

The purest blood in the world is that of a Christian ancestry. The Bible all through makes much of family descent. The true aristocracy is the aristocracy of grace. Cowper manfully exclaims:

> "My boast is not that I deduce my birth
> From loins enthroned, the rulers of the earth;
> But higher far my proud pretensions rise—
> The son of parents passed unto the skies."

The conceited coxcomb who talks disrespectfully of his parents, is ashamed to acknowledge his mother's prayers, and snaps his fingers at his father's instructions, is the silly fellow who invariably comes to a bad end. If you have come of a good stock, don't disgrace it. Keep up the noble succession—the only true succession—the line of saints.

MONEY ALL GONE.

"The fool and his money are soon parted." The prodigal son left home rich. His friends and acquaintances and flatterers declared with a "hip, hip, hurrah!" that he was the best fellow in the world. But we read: "And he began to be in want." Money all gone, and his friends were all gone. Such is the friendship of the world. As long as you have money and spend it liberally your generosity will be admired; you will be called the best fellow in the world, if you will only make a fool of yourself for other people's gratification; but as soon as your money is all gone, depend upon it, your friends will be gone too.

The prodigal son was at last compelled to feed swine. This, to the Jew, was the most scurvy work in which a man could engage. And how many men—*men* did I say?—excuse the mistake; how many swells, who live off the earnings of their fathers, if they were thrown upon their own resources, would be fit for no better employment than herding swine?

Young man, "the way of the transgressor is hard." The devil does not keep his promises; he is a cheat. The only wages he pays is degradation and damnation. Sin only degrades, diseases, bemeans, belittles, pauperizes, kills and damns!

THE CHRISTIAN CHARACTER.

The Christian should have a noble character: broad in his views and generous in his opinions. Bigotry makes man abominable wherever there is light, liberty or nobleness.

BORROWING TROUBLE.

Don't borrow trouble for the future. Half of the unhappiness in the world is caused by worrying over things which never happen.

A BASE MOTTO.

No Christian can adopt the motto "All is fair in trade." The Christian is a business man of conscious honor, integrity and high-mindedness.

THE JOYOUS CHRISTIAN.

Some Christians' faces look like midnight. They are as dispiriting as a funeral procession. The joyous Christian proclaims to the world that the Master he serves is a good one.

THE POOR.

Are you doing anything for the poor? You pity them, do you? For how much do you pity them?

ARITHMETIC.

Americans need to study arithmetic. If your income be $20 per week and your expenses $19—result, happiness. If your income be $20 and your expenses $21—result, misery.

WHEN IN ROME.

"When in Rome do as the Romans do." Never! There is no liberty in the man who, when in Rome, does not as he ought to do, but as the Romans do. There is no independence or manliness in that man. Doing as the Romans did ruined Rome.

HONESTY AND POLICY.

"Honesty is the best policy;" but he who is honest for policy's sake is not honest. Some men are honest when honesty pays; but when policy will serve them a better turn, they give honesty the slip and work policy.

AN ANTIDOTE FOR FRIVOLITY.

Culture is the best antidote for frivolity. We hear of dancing circles, etc. How many reading circles do the young women of high society maintain? Figures would present a sad commentary. Is it not sad that the feet should be educated at the expense of the head and heart?

A FALSE CHARITY.

Many people so divide the sermon out among the congregation that they keep none for themselves.

HASTY WORDS.

Dr. Fuller used to say that the heat of passion makes our souls to crack, and the devil creeps in at the crevices.

Says Lord Bacon: "An angry man who suppresses his passions, thinks worse than he speaks; and an angry man that will chide, speaks worse than he thinks."

WHY?

Why spend your money for strong drink? There are men who are shrewd in all their dealings, but will allow themselves to be cheated by unhealthy adulterations, and put an enemy to their mouths that will rob them of their senses.

GOOD-LOOKING FOLKS.

Good-looking people are mostly people lacking good sense. They have an idea that they were made to be looked at, and often they are good for nothing else. "Handsome is as handsome does."

HEAVEN UPON EARTH.

We often speak of heaven. We often desire it. We need not wait till we die to enjoy it. We may have heaven now. We can exhibit heavenly graces and dispositions. We can reflect the goodness and diffuse the mercy and kindness of heaven. Our pleasant looks, kind words, warm greetings and good deeds will create in each breast a little heaven.

THE FROSTED WINDOWS.

The frosted windows prove that the saloon-keeper is ashamed of his business. He is ashamed to let the world see the "blood-money" that goes over his counter. And a man that is ashamed of his business himself ought not to ask anybody else to have respect for it.

A SAD FACT.

It seems to be easier for a father to support six sons than it is for six sons to support a father; and easier for a mother to support six daughters than for six daughters to support a mother.

PLUCK.

Young man, be resolved to work your way through the world bravely and honestly. Luck is a fool; pluck is a hero. Pluck is the winning horse in the race of life. Have an objective point; have the back-bone to go after it, and then stick. And if you have not ambition enough to make a man of yourself and rise in the world, you might as well order your grave-clothes.

HOW TO DRIVE THE CHILDREN AWAY FROM HOME.

Reserve all your social charms for strangers abroad; be dull at home; don't talk; forbid your children to come into the nicely-furnished rooms; have no amusements and no pleasures; make home as irksome as possible; forget that you were once young—and your children will make every possible effort to get from home at night and run the streets.

DO RIGHT.

No man ever permanently suffered by a straight course of conduct. David never saw the righteous man forsaken, nor his children begging bread. We seldom do. It pays to be honest. It is safe to do right. The Lord looks grandly after the man who seeks to do right.

"THOU SHALT NOT STEAL."

This commandment not only forbids violent theft, but borrowing and forgetting to return, which is also stealing. Overhaul your hat and umbrella-stands, closets and book-shelves, and see if you have not borrowed some things which you have forgotten to return.

THE FALSE WITNESS.

False swearing is a gross crime. The lying witness does much hurt. He corrupts the judge; oppresses the innocent, suppresses the truth. He endangers the life, the liberty and all that is sacred to man. The false-witness bearer is the most vile and infamous, the most pernicious and perilous instrument of injustice; the most desperate enemy of man's right and safety that can be.

FIE FOR SHAME!

There are many men in this city, prominent in church and society, who rent their properties for saloons and houses of prostitution. I verily believe that some of these hypocrites would, for twenty-five per-cent. increase, rent their houses to the devil to start branch establishments of hell, if he would agree to furnish enough ice with which to cool the rent money—the price of blood. Fie for shame!

SHUT OUT.

When I was a boy, my mother once provided a singing-school teacher and books, and, though I had an ear and a voice, I would not go to school and learn music; and now that I can neither sing nor play, whose fault is it that I was never allowed to join a choir? Did the leader shut me out? I shut myself out. So, if I refuse God's gifts and shut myself out of heaven, I will have to blame myself, just as I now blame myself for my ignorance of music.

A GOOD CONSCIENCE.

Paul said before the Council: "*I have lived before God in all good conscience until this day.*" He thus plainly demonstrates from his own early experience that conscience is by no means an infallible guide. He served God in good conscience not only when he was St. Paul the apostle, but when he was Saul the persecutor. The sun-dial is an ingenious contrivance, but of no use when the sun does not shine. And so with a man's conscience: it is of use only when the Sun of Righteousness shines upon it.

SUNDAY AND THE WORKINGMAN.

The Sabbath is the great breakwater against oppressive monopolies. Sunday laws were first enacted in the interest of the laboring man by Constantine, the first Christian emperor. In opposing the Sunday laws, the workingmen of America are opening the way for employers to compel them at length to work seven days for six days' wages. Under existing Sunday laws, they get seven days' wages for six days' work.

"READY FOR EITHER."

We are too much like Redwald, the king of East Anglia, of whom it is said he had a picture of God on the one side of his shield and of Satan on the other, with the legend beneath: *Paratus ad utrum*—"ready for either."

THE COMMERCIAL LIAR.

Don't debauch your conscience. Tell the truth about your goods, though you may be discharged the next moment. You cannot afford to lie, cheat, deceive and swindle. At the bar of conscience the commercial lie is as bad as any other lie, and at the day of judgment the business liar will go down to death under as deep a condemnation as any other.

Tell the truth. Undoubtedly it is a hard thing for a man in business to tell the truth when it ought to be told. Tell the truth, no matter what is the custom of the trade—the established, acknowledged custom of the trade.

Even a white lie is a base, degrading thing. A lie is a lie. "*No man was ever lost in a straight road.*"

POLITICS AND RELIGION.

Christ laid down a great law of contact. Bring the Gospel into contact with society, its customs, its laws and its institutions. It will purge them of evil, elevate and refine them. The leaven of the Gospel is to be put into the political lump, and not to be kept as a thing apart from it, away from it, unmixed with it, but to affect, influence and regenerate it. Politics can only be made a pleasure and a profit by the infusion of Christian principles. The man who abjures politics is neither a good citizen nor a good Christian. Let the Christian conscience exert itself in politics, and mighty reforms will be brought about. The man who is opposed to mixing religion and politics generally has not the religion to mix— not the genuine article, which seeks to make this world wiser, happier and better.

"SEEK YE THE LORD."

"Seek ye the Lord." Why, is not God everywhere? Yes. Then he needs no seeking, for in him we live and move and have our being. This text does not so much refer as to where *God* is, as to where *you* are. You have turned your back on him; you have forgotten him; and so, because he has not been in your thoughts, you have, in a spiritual sense, lost the Lord. You are to realize that there is a God; your thought, love and desire are to come toward him, and thus you will find God.

A WISH.

There are many who, with a burdened heart, say: "*I wish I were a Christian!*" But all your wishing will never make you one. There is a great difference between *wishing* to be one and *choosing* to be one. A wish is not of itself a purpose. You may wish to go to Washington, but unless you act accordingly—unless you make your preparations, go to the depot and get your ticket, and, instead of sitting down in the depot and wishing yourself there, get aboard the train—*you will never get there.* So, if you want to go to the capital of the skies, you must get aboard the line of Christian influences that will bear you there.

WAITING.

But must I not wait till I am drawn? Wait for Him who has all these years been waiting for you? "Behold, I stand at the door and knock," cries the patient Saviour. It is he who is seeking you, and waiting for you, and not you for him. Why, he has been trying to bring you to him all these years: and now, instead of waiting to be "drawn" to the Father, *stop resisting*, and come.

INABILITY.

"I am unable to come; I am a sinner." That is just the reason why you are to come to Christ. You are not to stop on account of your sins, but seek the Lord *because* of them. Suppose the man with a withered hand, whom Christ met in the temple, when Christ bade him " Stretch it forth," had cried: "Stretch forth my hand? How can I? It is withered!" Of course his hand would never have been healed. But when he heard the command he obeyed. The same Being who bade him act gave him strength to act. That is just what you have to do. You hear the command. Obey it.

STUDY THE BIBLE.

Some men, when their consciences are aroused, run after catechisms, commentaries and systems. Love, faith and repentance first; theology next. Even Baxter's "Call to the Unconverted," or Alleine's "Alarm," are not what the anxious inquirer so much needs as the Word of the Lord. Here is the way, the truth and the life. This is the loudest call to the unconverted; this is the most fearful alarm to sinners. Study the Bible; therein are the words of eternal life.

TO BUSINESS MEN.

Religion is a man's chief business. You need not renounce the stirring business of temporal life to have eternal life. You need not neglect your business to take care of your soul. There is no antagonism between religion and business. Many men plead the pressure of their business as a reason for their little interest in things spiritual. But such men make God the author of a contradiction, for he has put man under the necessity of work, and under the necessity of divine worship. The doing of either cannot be injurious to the other. You can be successful in trade, wise in investments, and yet lay up treasures in heaven. In a few years it will be of little consequence whether you were rich or poor; but it will be of infinite consequence whether you were Christians or not.

A WORD TO THE AGED.

Many and solemn are the warnings which bid you prepare. Your wrinkled features, whitening hair and decaying strength loudly tell you that the end is near. You have reached three score years and ten. You are living upon borrowed time. Death comes striding after you with rapid steps! Judgment is close behind! But God loves you still. Though one foot be in the grave, you may have both feet on the Rock of Ages. Then you need not fear the closing hours of life. Christ will strengthen, cheer and comfort you, and your even-tide shall only be the prelude of a blessed morning—a morning without clouds.

COURTESY TO CHILDREN.

Many parents are wanting in courtesy to their children. They speak to them roughly, violently and insultingly, and so inflict painful wounds on their self-respect. Do not needlessly refer to their faults and follies. Be considerate. Never allude to the personal defects to which they are already keenly sensitive. Do not needlessly interfere with their plans, and impose on them unreasonable and fruitless sacrifices. Find as little fault with your children as possible, and praise them as much as you can.

TELL THE TRUTH.

Warburton says: "Lies have no legs and cannot stand;" but they have wings and can fly like a vampire. Lies go by telegraph; truth comes by mail one day late. Some one has said: "A big lie, like a big fish on dry land, will fret and fling, but will die of itself if left alone." The half-truth lies are the most dangerous of all lies. In Siam, a kingdom of Asia, he who is found guilty of telling a lie has his mouth sewed up. If we had such a law what a demand there would be for needles and thread!

"Buy the truth, and sell it not." To tell the truth at all times and under all circumstances, and in the face of all risks, requires more courage than was ever displayed upon the field of battle. Of all the valiant men in the world let him be chief who dares to tell the truth!

MIRTH A MEDICINE.

Solomon says: "A merry heart maketh a cheerful countenance, but by sorrow of the heart the spirit is broken." "Heaviness in the heart of man maketh it stoop, but a good word maketh it glad." "A merry heart doeth good like a medicine, but a broken spirit drieth the bones." Laughter, like a "thing of beauty," is "a joy forever."

"Laughter! 'tis the poor man's plaster,
Covering up each disaster;
Laughing, he forgets his troubles,
Which, though real, seem but bubbles;
Laughter, whether loud or mute,
Tells the human kind from brute;
Laughter! 'tis hope's living voice,
Bidding us to make a choice,
And to cull from thorny bowers,
Leaving thorns and taking flowers."

BEHIND THE AGE.

It is remarkable how many boys and girls on street-cars and railroads are behind the age.

A FACT.

The young man who will not cease drinking to please his sweetheart will never do so to please his wife. If you marry a man to mend him or reform him, you are a fool. Take no such chances.

BE YOUR OWN MATCH-MAKER.

Be your own match-maker. Depend on personal knowledge of the life and character of the individual who asks your hand and would link his life with yours. Marry into a family which you have long known.

A BAD MOTHER.

Fathers, unfortunately, as a rule are too busy in the rush of to-day's life to look after the religious training of the children. All depends upon the mother; and if the mother be a fool, then, alas! for the poor children.

LONG LIFE.

It is not the good but the bad that die young. Sin kills people. The psalmist says religion is "the saving health of the nations." You can find plenty of good old men, but bad old men are hard to find. "The wicked do not live out half their days."

LOYALTY TO CONSCIENCE.

Loyalty to conscience always did and always will give to the world its grandest benefactors.

PARTING WORDS.

I must stop now; for, if I have driven a nail in a sure place, I want to clinch it, and secure well the advantage, lest by hammering away I break the head off or split the board. When a woman was asked what she remembered of the minister's sermon, she said: "I recollect very little of it. It was about bad weights and short measures, and I did not recollect anything but to go home and burn the bushel." Promise me that you will do as much, and I will have written enough—for this time.

THE END.

www.ingramcontent.com/pod-product-compliance
Lightning Source LLC
Chambersburg PA
CBHW030243170426
43202CB00009B/606